Shared Dreams

Shared Dreams

Martin Luther King, Jr.
and the Jewish Community

RABBI MARC SCHNEIER

Preface by Martin Luther King III

JEWISH LIGHTS PUBLISHING
Woodstock, Vermont

Library of Congress Cataloging-in-Publication Data
Schneier, Marc, 1959–
Shared dreams: Martin Luther King, Jr. and the Jewish community / by Marc Schneier ;
preface by Martin Luther King III.
p.   cm.
Includes index.
ISBN 1-58023-062-8 (hardcover)
1. King, Martin Luther, Jr., 1929–1968—Relations with Jews. 2. Afro-Americans—Civil
rights—History—20th century. 3. Jews—Civil rights—United States—History—20th
century. 4. Afro-Americans—Relations with Jews. 5. Civil rights movements—United
States—History—20th century. 6. United States—Race relations. I. Title.

E185.97.K5 S595 1999
323'.092—dc21

99-046047

First Edition

10   9   8   7   6   5   4   3   2   1

Manufactured in the United States of America

Cover design: Drena Fagen
Text design: Susan Ramundo

Published by Jewish Lights Publishing
A Division of LongHill Partners, Inc.
Sunset Farm Offices, Route 4
P.O. Box 237
Woodstock, Vermont 05091
Tel: (802) 457-4000   Fax: (802) 457-4004
www.jewishlights.com

To my beloved wife, Toby,
and our children, Sloane and Brendan

Contents

Acknowledgments		viii
Preface by Martin Luther King III		xi
Introduction		xiii
1	The "New Moses"	1
2	"Cease to Do Evil, Learn to Do Good": Jewish Tradition and Social Justice	11
3	The Updated Covenant	19
4	"Out of Zion Shall Go Forth the Law": King and the Jews	29
5	Montgomery: The Journey Begins	37
6	A Refugee from the "Commercial Jungle": Stanley Levison	49
7	"Moses" Returns to Atlanta	57
8	"Only Rabble-Rousers Recite Psalms with Negroes"	69
9	"Raging" Bull: Hell in Birmingham	77
10	All Eyes on Washington	93
11	Freedom Summer, 1964	99
12	"Our Marching Steps Will Thunder: We Survive!"	107
13	A Poisoned Fountain: St. Augustine	121
14	A Kindred Spirit: Abraham Joshua Heschel	133
15	Selma: The Ultimate Freedom March	145
16	Afrocentrists' New Target: Israel	159
17	Friendship Lost	171
18	From One Battle to Another	181
19	End of the Dream: Memphis	189
Epilogue		193
Notes		196
Index		216

Acknowledgments

Permit me to thank the following for their friendship and wise counsel: Elan Steinberg, Israel Singer, Kweisi Mfume, Hugh Price, S. Daniel Abraham, Congressman Charles Rangel and Ken Sunshine. I am grateful to my beloved friend Martin Luther King III for his impassioned preface. My deepest appreciation to him and to Gwen Blount for her assistance.

I must remember my co-founder of The Foundation for Ethnic Understanding, a true visionary in the field of racial harmony, the late Joseph Papp. His wife, Gail, continues to devote her time, energy and resources to our landmark work. I salute my fellow officers at The Foundation: Darwin Davis, Stephanie Shnay, Edward Yardeni, and Robert Cyruli for their dedication and deep commitment to the furthering of Black/Jewish relations. To Lawrence Kopp, Executive Director, and Meredith Flug, Deputy Executive Director, my gratitude for their honest professional advice, useful comments, and editorial help.

The following must be singled out for their support and assistance in making this book a reality: my research editor, Phil Sieradski, whose extensive interviews enabled me to make this story a reality, my editor, Arthur Magida, whose suggestions for organizing and presenting the material steered the book to completion, Robert Youdelman and Pam Bernstein, who helped me navigate the world of publishing, my friends at Jewish Lights Publishing, Stuart Matlins and Sandra Korinchak, for their conviction, patience, and deeply held commitment to this project, and Amy Rubin, Michael Gelb and Gene Rubin, who contributed invaluable research.

Research for this book would not have been possible without the support of the Samuel Bronfman Foundation. My thanks for their generosity, which has brought to life this previously untold story of mutual support and cooperation.

Glenn Dorskind generously read the manuscript and shared his comments with me. Additional help came from my friends and colleagues, Rabbi Jay Rosenbaum and Rabbi Gilbert S. Rosenthal.

As always, my beloved congregation, The Hampton Synagogue, has been a constant source of strength and encouragement to my vision of tolerance, human dignity and human rights. I must single out the synagogue's officers: Michael Weisbrod, Martin Berman, Seymour Siegel, and Gerald Rausnitz, for their love and support.

Lastly and most importantly, my heart goes out to my beloved wife, Toby, my light and inspiration, who shares in my dreams. May our children, Sloane and Brendan, grow up to live in a world free of discrimination and bigotry.

Preface

I will never forget my first introduction to the work of Rabbi
Marc Schneier and the Foundation for Ethnic Understanding. I
had just been named the fourth president of the Southern Christian
Leadership Conference, the organization co-founded by my father,
Martin Luther King, Jr. One of the first letters of congratulations
was from Rabbi Schneier. It included an invitation to speak on the
state of Black/Jewish relations in the United States at Yeshiva
University.

A friendship grew from that invitation. As I interacted more with
Rabbi Schneier and learned more about the work of the Foundation,
I learned that Rabbi Schneier had a burning desire to advance relations between our respective races. Moreover, as a man of God, he
was convinced that while we may have respective differences in our
communities, we had much more in common as part of the brotherhood of man.

My discussions with my friend, Rabbi Schneier, often centered around the American civil rights movement and the work of my father. I was impressed that Marc not only knew intimately the history of my father's work with the civil rights movement, he was also well-versed in the history of my father's connections to the Jewish community. In time, he revealed that he had devoted much time and energy to research of the two.

Shared Dreams is the culmination of that effort. While much has been written about the work of my father, Rabbi Schneier has gone to great lengths to compile the complex story of the cooperation, and sometimes angst, between blacks and Jews during the civil rights movement in the context of Martin Luther King, Jr.'s life. From the account of his friendship with men like the incomparable Rabbi Abraham Joshua Heschel and his advisers, Stanley Levison and Harry Wachtel, to anti-Semitic sentiments within the movement itself, Rabbi Schneier examines different aspects of the relation between my father and the Jewish community. As such, he outlines a compelling image of relations between the two communities.

The history of Americans of African descent and Jewish descent is a story of two groups of people who have suffered uncommon persecution but who have persevered with uncommon faith. This is our common ground. We share the dream of a beloved community where one can live without the threat of racism, poverty, or violence. We share the dream of a beloved community where the worst of the human spirit is defeated by our best. In *Shared Dreams*, Rabbi Schneier reiterates our commonality, as upheld by Martin Luther King, Jr., and fuels the reader to continue to work for the advancement of race relations among all God's children.

— Martin Luther King III

Introduction

Much has been written about that time when a movement came into being whose goal was to free African Americans from discrimination and racism. Though blacks were the prime architects of this movement that was founded on religion and faith and hope, the battle for freedom would have taken longer—and been even more torturous—if not for the participation of people who were not blacks and who put their own lives on the line to help African Americans. Only after middle-class whites, especially ministers, priests, and rabbis, began participating in civil rights demonstrations did the movement gain the attention that was needed to pass the landmark civil rights legislation of 1964 and 1965.

No black figure of the period received as much allegiance from people sympathetic to civil rights as did Martin Luther King, Jr. And no segment of the white community provided as much—and as consistent—support for King as did the Jewish community. Jewish support for King and for civil rights is fairly widely known. It is a story worth telling fully, and that is done here in relation to Dr. King and his efforts. But little has been told about King's support for issues that almost exclusively concerned the Jewish community, such as easing discrimination against Jews in the Soviet Union and assuring the safety and security of the State of Israel. He also spoke out against anti-Semitism in the United States, especially when that virus erupted among blacks. King did not often have the opportunity to express his ongoing support of the Jewish community because he was almost wholly consumed—as he should have been—with the fight for blacks to secure full human rights in this country. But the fact that there was, even sporadically, a two-way street between King and the Jewish community is both impressive and surprising. King did what he could for the Jewish people within the limits of his role as an advocate for his own people, and within the limits of his own political and moral power. He understood that a people who fought for their rights were only as honorable as was their concern for the rights of all people.

Jews should be proud of their participation in the civil rights struggle. They should hold that up as an inspiration to all generations: it is emblematic of what the sages call *tikkun olam*, the mandate for Jews to repair the world, to make it whole and move it closer to a messianic age of truth and compassion. We hope that the story told here will encourage Jewish people and people of all faiths in such efforts in the future.

But King's reciprocation shows his full humanity and also inspires us, especially since, given the historical circumstances of the time and the discrepancies in power between the black and Jewish communities, it was hardly surprising that Jews' assistance to blacks was greater than what blacks were doing for Jews. And also since, by reciprocating, he risked opprobrium from fellow blacks, particularly as Black Power, with its shadings of anti-Zionism and anti-Semitism,

was on the upswing. His empathy and outspokenness show the brav-
ery—and the firmness—of his conscience, and the reality of his
"dream." This dream was as rooted in the Jewish idea of *tikkun olam*
as it was in the Baptist vineyards where King preached and prayed,
and where he did his work for God in the terrible, yet glorious battle-
fields of Selma and Birmingham. And most sadly, of course, in
Memphis, after which it was up to the world to repair itself for the terrible deed done against this man who had struggled so hard, as had
the prophet Amos (5:24), for "justice to roll down like waters, and
righteousness like a mighty stream."

The "New Moses"

To avoid involvement in behalf of a just cause . . . is to live a sterile life. It is the quality of life that one leads that gives it meaning and value, not its length. From the saying of Jesus: "He that loseth his life for my sake shall find it," I draw the fullest meaning and implication for my life. . . . The exhortation of the prophet, "Justice, justice, shalt thou pursue," rings constantly in my ears.

—MARTIN LUTHER KING, JR.

I t is now more than thirty years since the death of Martin Luther King, Jr. King was brought up by a father who had been a pastor. He had trained to be a pastor. He started out in life as a pastor. Almost by accident, he entered a public arena that took him far from his pulpit and his congregants in Montgomery, Alabama. Yet, despite his reluctance to start out on this road, despite his occasional bewilderment that he had become a "new Moses" for his people, he led a revolution that changed the social structure of America and how America thought about itself and how it showed itself to the rest of the world.

He was born Michael King on January 15, 1929, in Atlanta, Georgia; his name was formally changed to Martin Luther King, Jr., some six years later. His mother, Alberta Williams, was the daughter of Rev. Adam Daniel Williams, pastor of the Ebenezer Baptist Church in Atlanta and founder of the Atlanta chapter of the National Association for the Advancement of Colored People (NAACP). When Williams died in 1931, he was succeeded in his church pulpit by his son-in-law, Rev. Martin Luther King, Sr. One of the early combatants in the war of discrimination against blacks, Martin Luther King, Sr., also known as Daddy King, was a proud and ambitious man, who labored hard in the fields of his religion. In addition to Martin Jr., Daddy King and his wife had two other children: Christine and Albert Daniel.

The King household was loving and comparatively well-to-do. Not until Martin Jr. began to attend the Younge Street Grade School did he really experience discrimination: White children he had played with in his neighborhood were no longer allowed to play with him. Growing up with America at war in Europe and the Pacific, King attended a special accelerated program at the University of Atlanta, then returned to Booker T. Washington High School to graduate in 1944. At the age of fifteen, he enrolled at Morehouse College. He was undecided about a future career and considering law and teaching as possibilities, but he felt no pull toward the ministry. Rejecting the religious emotionalism of the church and its literal interpretations of scripture, he favored liberal European-American theological and philosophical ideas.[1]

King's exposure to Morehouse President Benjamin Mays and the Christian social activism espoused by his teachers—and his own readings of the theologians Paul Tillich, Henry Nelson Wieman, Walter

Rauschenbusch, and Reinhold Niebuhr—caused him to change his mind and enter the ministry. He was ordained in 1947. His father quickly helped him become assistant pastor of Ebenezer, though he was still a student at college.

In 1948, King graduated from Morehouse and went on to Crozer Theological Seminary in Chester, Pennsylvania, where he was one of six blacks in a student body of 100. At Crozer, his preaching skills helped make him a standout: he was elected president of the student body, honored with the Pflaker Award as outstanding student, and given the J. Lewis Crozer Fellowship. After graduating in 1951, he used his fellowship to attend Boston University's School of Theology, where he received his Ph.D. in systematic theology in 1955.

While a student at Boston University, he met Coretta Scott, a music student who was active in social movements and shared King's pacifist views. He married her on June 18, 1953, at her family's home in Marion, Alabama. Around that same time he accepted the position of pastor of the Dexter Avenue Baptist Church in Montgomery, Alabama. From the very beginning, he preached to parishioners about the importance of registering to vote, about being involved in community affairs and the need to join the NAACP.

The South was about to undergo some major upheavals. Blacks, oppressed since being brought here from Africa to be slaves, had been kept down after the Civil War by a raft of new laws passed during Reconstruction. In 1896, the Supreme Court ruling in *Plessy v. Ferguson* introduced a new legal concept, "separate but equal," which was applied to the continuation of segregation in public schools. Though black schools were supposed to receive funding, physical plants, and staffs all equivalent to those given to white schools, black children actually received vastly inferior educations than did whites because neither the quality nor the quantity of funding, buildings, and staffs for them ever came close to what white children enjoyed.

In 1951, the NAACP filed a class action suit to overturn the *Plessy* decision. Combining several national cases, the overall suit came to be called *Brown v. Board of Education (of Topeka, Kansas)*. In 1954, the Supreme Court ruled that "separate but equal" was unconstitutional because it deprived blacks of the equal protection of the laws guaranteed by the Fourteenth Amendment.[2]

The decision ignited a social revolution as well as a vitriolic backlash in the South:

> White Southerners were shocked by *Brown*. Many predicted violence or even a new attempt by southern states to secede from the union if the federal government attempted to make good on the Court's ruling. The day of the [Supreme Court's] decision—May 17, 1954— became known as Black Monday. In rural Sunflower County, Mississippi, a former Mississippi State football hero named Robert "Tut" Patterson, finding himself so tormented by the implications of *Brown* for his young daughters that he could not sleep at night, set to work to form the first chapter of the Citizens' Council, a segregationist committee of white businessmen. Within two years [the Council had] 85,000 members in Mississippi and 60,000 in Alabama as well as countless chapters across the South from Texas to Virginia. . . . [I]n an atmosphere of mounting hysteria, southern politicians assured their constituents that forced integration would never come.[3]

On December 1, 1955, America's second revolutionary shot was "heard 'round the world." In Montgomery, Alabama, Mrs. Rosa Parks was ordered to give her seat on a bus to a white person. She refused. Her act of defiance, resulting in her arrest, sparked the creation of the Montgomery Improvement Association, which organized a bus boycott that lasted 382 days. Though not wanting a leadership role, Martin Luther King, Jr., was induced to become its president. "We were just looking for an agreeable figurehead," said Montgomery leader E. D. Nixon later, "and we got a Moses."[4]

The year 1956 was pivotal in King's life. He was arrested for the first time on January 26 for speeding. Four days later, his home was bombed. Through it all, King adopted the Gandhian philosophy of passive resistance, hoping it would

> not "defeat or humiliate" the opponent but [also] "awaken a sense of moral shame in the opponent" and thereby create "the beloved community." [H]e [also] distinguished between seeking to defeat the "forces of evil" and "persons victimized by evil" [and lastly he] asserted that the underlying principle of nonviolent resistance was "agape"—that is, "an overflowing love which seeks nothing in return." This principle enabled King to merge Gandhian precepts with his Christian beliefs: "When we love on the agape level we love men not because we like them, not because their attitudes and ways appeal to us, but because God loves them."[5]

In November, the Supreme Court upheld a lower court's ruling that segregation on buses in Montgomery was unconstitutional. A few weeks later, Martin Luther King was one of the first to board an unsegregated bus.

As the bus boycott received national attention, King became a hero of the nascent civil rights movement. A star had been born, a new Moses had arisen, who would lead his people out of bondage. And so, in January 1957, Southern black leaders converged on Ebenezer Baptist Church to form a new resistance movement—the Southern Christian Leadership Conference (SCLC). King was made its first president. That year, he traveled almost a million miles and delivered about two hundred speeches. In March, he traveled to Ghana as a guest of the new government and completed his first book, *Stride Toward Freedom*, published in 1958.

Because of the new demands on him, King realized that he could no longer fulfill his commitments to his congregation in

Montgomery. Resigning his position at Dexter, he moved back to Atlanta and resumed a co-pastorship with his father of the Ebenezer Baptist Church.

Now that King had a center-stage position in the black freedom movement, the State of Alabama took an overly enthusiastic look at him, his friends, and his finances. In 1960, a Montgomery grand jury indicted him for falsifying his tax returns. But the attention of the Federal government would be even more intense. J. Edgar Hoover, director of the FBI, took a special interest in King after the minister chided the FBI for having no black agents. For the imperious Hoover, this was a personal attack. Through wiretaps, listening devices, and actual physical surveillance, Hoover documented King's SCLC activities, personal conversations, dalliances, and the conversations of friends and associates. Hoover would harass King for the rest of his life, even suggesting that King commit suicide before "improprieties" were revealed.

As the civil rights movement's tactics changed from economic boycotts to sit-ins and freedom rides and marches that were easy targets for the tear gas and fire hoses of police and state troopers, King met with President John F. Kennedy in the White House in October 1962 to press for more federal action for civil rights.

Arrested at yet another demonstration in April 1963—this time in Birmingham, Alabama—King used his time in jail to write "Letter from Birmingham City Jail," which would become a key document of the Negro revolution. His experiences in Birmingham became the essence of his next book, *Why We Can't Wait* (1964).

Birmingham marked a seminal change in America's view of blacks. After seeing newspaper and television images of protesters— men, women, and children—being attacked by dogs, water hoses, and baton-swinging police, a growing sympathy for blacks encouraged more whites to participate in the civil rights movement. Partly because of that, more than 250,000 people—blacks *and* whites—converged on Washington on August 28, 1963, for what would be the largest civil rights protest ever held in the United States.

On the steps of the Lincoln Memorial, King delivered one of the most inspiring speeches of all time:

> Five score years ago, a great American, in whose symbolic shadow we stand, signed the Emancipation Proclamation. This momentous decree came as a great beacon light of hope to millions of Negro slaves who had been seared in the flames of withering injustice. It came as a joyous daybreak to end the long night of captivity.
>
> But one hundred years later, the Negro is still not free; one hundred years later, the life of the Negro is still sadly crippled by the manacles of segregation and the chains of discrimination; one hundred years later, the Negro lives on a lonely island of poverty in the midst of a vast ocean of material prosperity; one hundred years later, the Negro is still languishing in the corners of American society and finds himself an exile in his own land. So we have come here today to dramatize a shameful condition.[6]

"From every mountainside," pleaded King, "let freedom ring. . . . If America is to be a great nation, this must be true. So let freedom ring." King oratorically went from state to state and coast to coast, tolling the bells of freedom and envisioning "that day when *all* God's children, black men and white men, Jews and gentiles, Protestants and Catholics, will be able to join hands and sing in the words of the old Negro spiritual, 'Free at last! Free at last! Thank God Almighty, we are free at last!'"

In December, *Time* magazine anointed King Man of the Year. But only when Lyndon Johnson became president after John Kennedy was assassinated in November 1963 did civil rights move close to the forefront of the White House's priorities. Johnson deemed it time for a Great Society to emerge in America, one in which poverty would be eradicated, opportunities would expand, and blacks would have equal rights and equal opportunity. Many blacks assumed this was the beginning of a new era.

The summer of 1964 saw the passage of a national civil rights bill, but it was not enough to quell the riots that broke out in Northern cities. In July, the SCLC launched a people-to-people tour of Mississippi to help sister groups—the Student Nonviolent Coordinating Committee (SNCC) and the Congress of Racial Equality (CORE)—get Negro voters to register. The campaign was called the Mississippi Freedom Summer.

Also in 1964, for the first time, King came out in favor of a political candidate: Lyndon Johnson. King was appalled by the regressive politics of the GOP's presidential candidate, Arizona Senator Barry Goldwater, and he appreciated the president's efforts to advance civil rights legislation. In October, after returning from a special audience with Pope Paul VI in Rome, King learned that he had won the 1964 Nobel Peace Prize.

In January 1965, while leading a voter registration drive in Selma called Project Alabama, King was jailed after leading a protest march to the Dallas County Courthouse. In February, he met in the White House with President Johnson, who assured him that he would do his utmost to ensure Negro voting rights. In March, King again gained national attention when he led the Selma-to-Montgomery march. In July, thirty thousand people marched for civil rights in Chicago, where King was stoned by counter-protesters for involving himself in Northern affairs. Early in August, King went to Washington to attend the culmination of years of work: the signing of the Voting Rights Act. At last, one of his fondest dreams had become law.

During this time, King concluded that the war in Vietnam was unjust and publicly announced his opposition. He said, "I knew that

I could never again raise my voice against the violence of the oppressed in the ghettoes without having first spoken clearly to the greatest purveyor of violence in the world today—my own government."[7]

This began a downward spiral in King's influence. His opposition to the Vietnam War divided supporters who were upset that he
seemed to be mixing two different matters—war and civil rights—
under one mantle. It also brought to the fore more radical, more violent black groups when members scorned King's nonviolence.
Seeking to give whites pain and anguish similar to what they had
inflicted on blacks, they advocated Black Power and separatism. As a
result, financial support waned for the SCLC and other leading civil
rights organizations.

On April 4, 1967, King spoke at The Riverside Church, an inter-
denominational church, in New York City. Amid clergy, scholars, and
other opponents of the war in Vietnam, he declared:

> These are revolutionary times. All over the globe men are revolting
> against old systems of exploitation and oppression, and out of the
> wombs of a frail world new systems of justice and equality are being
> born. . . . Every nation must now develop an overriding loyalty to
> mankind as a whole. . . . When I speak of love I am not speaking of
> some sentimental and weak response . . . [but] of that force which all
> of the great religions have seen as the supreme unifying principle of
> life. . . . Let us hope that this spirit will become the order of the day.[8]

On March 28, 1968, despite warnings of danger, King led six
thousand protesters in Memphis in support of the city's striking sanitation workers. Six days later, he delivered his "I've Been to the
Mountaintop" speech at a rally for the strikers:

> Well, I don't know what will happen now. We've got some difficult
> days ahead. But it doesn't matter with me now. Because I've been to

the mountaintop. And I don't mind. Like anybody, I would like to live a long life. Longevity has its place. But I'm not concerned about that now. I just want to do God's will. And He's allowed me to go up to the mountain. And I've looked over. And I've seen the promised land. I may not get there with you. But I want you to know tonight, that we, as a people will get to the promised land. And I'm happy, tonight. I'm not worried about anything. I'm not fearing any man. Mine eyes have seen the glory of the coming of the Lord.[9]

The next day—April 4, 1968—an assassin's bullet ended King's life. Cities burned and ghettoes exploded. "Moses" was gone. The man whose eyes had seen the glory of the coming of the Lord was now in the hands of the Lord. But his dream didn't die with him—a dream of the "day when *all* God's children . . . will . . . join hands and sing, . . . 'Free at last! Free at last! Thank God Almighty, we are free at last!'" The death of his dream would take more than bullets from an assassin, more than the death of one man. It would require the death of the entire American experiment—and the American promise—of democracy and freedom and equality. King's greatest gift was that the words of the prophet, "Justice, justice, shalt thou pursue," rang constantly in his ears, as did the words of the Constitution, "to form a more perfect Union." Through justice, King wanted to better the United States, maybe not to make it perfect—that is too ideal a goal for any institution made by human beings. But he never ceased trying to remind us that we should *reach* for perfection, however elusive that might be. And that by reaching, we would be a finer nation and a finer people.

2

"Cease to Do Evil, Learn to Do Good": Jewish Tradition and Social Justice

When Jews began marching with Dr. King, they invariably justified their participation with the statement that they were Jews and had an obligation to help. But what was that obligation and where did it come from? A brief overview of Jewish law and custom might help us understand.

Jewish concern about all people is founded in a tradition that started long before Moses climbed Mount Sinai to receive the Ten Commandments. "Why did God choose to create mankind from one man instead of from many?' asks the Talmud. And the Rabbis reply, 'So that no man might boast that his father is descended from better ancestry, although no two men are alike.'"[1]

In 1964, when the civil rights movement was cresting, Rabbi Israel Gerber wrote an essay in *Jewish Heritage* magazine on "the meaning of freedom" in which he attributed Jews' pursuit of social justice to the all-pervasive idea of monotheism. Oneness applied not only to God but to the entire human race:

Monotheism, the belief in the existence of One God who is the Creator and Sustainer of the universe, established the foundation for the democratic idea: since there is but one God, and since He created man in His own image, then all men are equally His children. The concept of One God embraces the equality of all men. Possessing a divine spark within him, each human being, regardless of station, deserves equal consideration and respect. From its inception, the Jewish people has held as basic concerns the dignity of the individual, protection of his rights and development of his abilities.[2]

With this belief in the dignity of man came the concept of justice: there can be no dignity if all is not right with all men, all women, all children. As the eminent rabbi Leo Baeck wrote:

One can not understand the place that justice has in the Bible without knowing that it always means revelation. Judaism does not know, in the strict sense of the word, the revealed God. He remains always the hidden, secret and mysterious God. But there is one revelation— the revelation of "Thou shalt not" and "Thou shalt," which means "do justice" in the full sense of the word. And this is what revelation is.[3]

As we delve into the Bible, that commandment to do what is right is reinforced again and again. As the prophet Isaiah proclaimed: "Cease to do evil, learn to do good; seek justice, correct oppression" (Isaiah 1:16–17). Much of Hebraic law and interpretation specifically concerns a Jew's relationship with a fellow Jew or a proselyte. But love and respect for a non-Jew is also important. "You shall love your neighbor as yourself" the Bible declares in Leviticus 19:18, but equally important is that you help those in need. The *mitzvah* (commandment) of *pidyon shvuyim*, the ransoming of a captive, is an example of that duty to another:

He who neglects the *mitzvah* of *pidyon shvuyim* transgresses the following: "Do not harden your heart and shut your hand against your

needy kinsman" (Deuteronomy 15:7); ..."Do not profit by the blood
of your neighbor" (Leviticus 19:16) ... Every moment that one delays
redeeming captives, it is as if he has spilled blood. [*Yoreh Deah* 252][4]

Because it is written in Exodus 23:9, "You shall not oppress a
stranger; you know the heart of a stranger, for you were strangers in
the land of Egypt," it was then no reach for *pidyon shevuyim* to
encompass "the idea of using political influence on behalf of beleaguered communities."[5]

And so, throughout biblical history, the Hebrew prophets followed the word of God and railed against the injustices of "man's
inhumanity to man." Or, as theologian and Holocaust survivor Emil
Fackenheim has put it:

If there is a single religious affirmation which, first coming with Judaism
into the world, has remained basic to Jewish belief until today, it is that
the God on high loves widows and orphans below; and that He com-
mands men, from on high, to do His will in the social order below.
Elsewhere, too, men have had an awareness of the Divine, and a
sense of responsibility in the social realm. It was the distinctive contribution of the Hebrew prophets to proclaim that the two cannot
be rent apart; that men ought to treat each other as created in the
image of a God who challenges them to this task.[6]

So it can be seen that the love of one's fellow human being has
long been central to Jewish belief. From this framework, the rabbis
found a rationale for their civil rights work. As Rabbi Bernard
Mandelbaum, president of The Jewish Theological Seminary of
America, wrote:

Jewish law stresses our duty to become involved. It is written in
Scripture: "When someone is in a position to testify about [an evil]
he has seen or learned of [on good authority] and he does not, he is

subject to punishment" (Leviticus 5:1). Tradition makes it clear that the punishment referred to is not one meted out by man, but by God. Failure to "get involved," to be helpful in righting a wrong, is the infraction of a moral duty for which man must answer to God and his inner conscience. "For without such involvement ["testimony"] society cannot continue to exist . . . the basis of this commandment is its indispensability for all mankind. The reasons for this need not be elaborated, for it should he self-evident to anyone who sees the light of day."[7]

But for many Jews, being involved with civil disobedience and protest might appear to conflict with the biblical concept of rendering unto Caesar what was Caesar's. In the daily prayer book, Jews offer allegiance to their country: "Deepen our love for our country and our desire to serve it. Strengthen our power of self-sacrifice for our nation's welfare. Teach us to uphold its good name by our right conduct. Cause us to see clearly that the well-being of our nation is in the hands of all its citizens. . . ." So what does a Jew do when social responsibility requires that he or she violate that allegiance to civil order?

As Rabbi Everett Gendler, who was active in the civil rights movement, wrote: "Judaism is highly respectful of duly constituted authority, [but] this does not absolve the individual from the duty of making responsible moral decisions."[8]

Many instances could be cited of disobedience to established authority, whether Jewish or non-Jewish, where such authority violated the basic moral and religious convictions of Judaism. Abraham, Moses, Elijah, Jeremiah, Shimon bar Yochai, Jochanan ben Zakkai, etc., are the heroes of numerous tales and legends lauding their refusals to obey illicit authority and unjust laws. . . . [A] well-established principle of Talmudic law is: "There is no agent for a sinful act." This is held to mean that a responsible adult cannot evade the legal consequences of the act committed by pleading that he was "merely following orders."

More precisely, in the opinion of the Talmud he is guilty of following the wrong orders: "If there is a conflict between the words of
the Master (God) and the words of the student (man), whose are to
be obeyed?"[9]

Therefore, for a Jew to be involved in an act of civil disobedience
is not only permissible under Judaic law but required by the word of
God. "It should be obvious," wrote Samuel Broude,

that as citizens of this country, and as adherents to Judaism, we have
obligations to both. As long as these two claims on our loyalty do not
pull in opposite directions, there is no problem. But when "the law of
the land" outrages our Jewish conscience, when the law of the state
permits discrimination against a group within the community or
against a single individual, then it is our duty to protest even if we
must break the law to do so. Dina d'malchuta dina ["The law of the
land is the law"—a Jewish legal maxim] was never intended to legit-
imize the civil government under any circumstances, but only under
conditions which do not undermine the proper expression of
Judaism. Dina d'malchuta dina permits us to participate in day-to-day
citizenship, but not to deny God or His commandments.[10]

Clearly, Jewish theology and history—indeed, the very commandments of God—almost require that Jews help others. But there
is more—and here is where the involvement of Jewish people with
civil rights becomes most intriguing, if not slightly perplexing: The
majority of those Jews who went South to help blacks or who demonstrated in their own communities or gave money to the movement
were neither rabbis nor adherents of Orthodoxy. It was just the opposite. In fact: most Jews who participated in the movement were the
least religious of Jews. Though the Torah seems clear—

I am the LORD, I have called you in righteousness, I have taken you
by the hand and kept you; I have appointed you as a covenant to the

> people, as a light to the nations, to open the eyes that are blind, to bring out the prisoners from the dungeon, and from the prison those who sit in darkness. (Isaiah 42:6–7)

—it would not be the most traditionally observant Jews who would be in the forefront in helping blacks get justice. Instead of Orthodox Jews leading the way, it was Reform and Conservative Jews, as well as those who were not affiliated with any movement within Judaism.

This strange dichotomy has defined Jews throughout history. Though the Torah and its commentaries provide ample guidelines for Jewish action, most often it has been those Jews who are not traditionally observant who have championed the social justice that is so emblematic of a Jewish ethos. Throughout history, it has been secular Jews and those involved in the progressive Jewish religious movements—those dedicated to liberal political and social ideals—who have moved beyond insularity to help those outside their faith. Jewish involvement in the civil rights movement became yet another example of these social, political, and religious traditions—traditions that were matters of conscience as well as faith, more a matter of seeking justice as the prophets instructed rather than adhering to a set of religious laws, *halakhah*. As Peter Orris, a Harvard freshman at the time, said of his participation in civil rights, "I had been raised in a family where being Jewish was important in terms of identifying with the underdog, with people who were suffering repression and discrimination."[11] The same applied to the many Jews who gave their money, their time, their intellect and their emotions to the civil rights movement—and the few who gave their lives.

But were those who were involved more Jewishly attuned than they knew? There is no easy way to know why people do what they do. Psychologists have been trying to answer those questions for a hundred years. But throughout history, Jews' beliefs and actions have often made them stand apart from others. Somewhere, buried in the Jewish collective unconscious and burnished in the Jewish soul, is that duty to be a light unto the nations. So it was the emphasis given to social justice by Jewish law and customs that was heard so clearly throughout the civil rights era by Jews who came from the more liberal Jewish denominations, or from no denomination at all.

3

The Updated Covenant

Throughout American history, the skin color of blacks has marked them as outsiders and strangers in their own country. Even in their devotion to God, they have been different from most of white America: The ecstatic nature of their services are in sharp contrast to whites' more sedate, more restrained worship. This has often made them seem even more alien, more odd, more representative of the "other" than they might have been otherwise. Though as human beings they were entitled to the same rights, respect, and consideration due to any people, American society singled them out for pariah status.

The eternal pariah, the Jew, could not help but feel some bond with yet another victim of hatred and discrimination. But what inducement was there for Jews to dedicate themselves to the black cause? With educational demands, economic and social constraints, and concern for the often-troubled, often-endangered State of Israel calling them, why should Jews extend themselves and even risk their lives for black social justice? Yet, in the United States where Jews were just two percent of the entire population, half to two-thirds of the whites who participated in the civil rights movement were Jews.[1]

The relationship between Jews and blacks dates back to the days of the Hebrews. The forefathers of Abraham were the dark-skinned Cushites. Moses had no difficulty passing himself off as an olive-skinned Egyptian, and his wife, Tzipporah, was a woman of color. The line between Jews and darker-skinned people was pliable and porous—and often it completely disappeared.

As early as 1948, James Baldwin had written in an essay entitled "The Harlem Ghetto," which appeared in *Commentary* when it was still published by the American Jewish Committee:

> [T]he Negro identifies himself almost wholly with the Jew. The more devout Negro considers that he *is* a Jew, in bondage to a hard taskmaster and waiting for a Moses to lead him out of Egypt. The hymns, the texts, and the most favored legends of the devout Negro are all Old Testament and therefore Jewish in origin: the flight from Egypt, the Hebrew children in the fiery furnace, the terrible jubilee songs of deliverance. . . . The covenant God made in the beginning with Abraham and which was to extend to his children and to his children's children forever is a covenant made with these latter-day exiles also: as Israel was chosen, so are they.[2]

History has shown that there have been more coalitions and alliances between blacks and Jews in the United States than between any two other peoples. Nevertheless, the history of Jewish involvement with American blacks has always involved a certain dichotomy. On the one hand, though *tzedakah* (charity) and *gemilut chassadim* (loving kindness) are Jewish *mitzvot* (commandments) to which almost all Jews subscribe, helping blacks achieve a better life was seen as politically and socially beneficial for the Jew as well, possibly because blacks and Jews have shared a position in American society unlike that of any other social groups. Though all newcomers have been discriminated against in their climb up the American social ladder, no other two groups have such a remarkable history in America. Especially at the beginning of the twentieth century, their work together—and particularly Jewish empathy for blacks—came from centuries of being victims.

> While many of the Socialist-Zionist immigrants were not sophisticated ideologues, even the least sophisticated or ideological among them deeply believed that discrimination and persecution were evils and that blacks, like Jews in Eastern Europe, suffered from a deep, economically based, and racially motivated hatred that had to be opposed. The idea of an alliance between Jews and blacks was a central tenet of all left-wing and liberal American Jews. In the early 1920s the Yiddish press regularly condemned American racism as it affected blacks. Jews then could not have helped identifying what America did to blacks with what Europe, and to considerable extent America, was doing to Jews.[3]

But the position of Jews and blacks in America had set them down different paths from each other. Even from their first days in the New World, Jews were able to assimilate into the white society, whereas blacks could not. Jews pulled themselves up by their bootstraps, while blacks didn't even have boots to pull up. And Jews had a social and family unity that bound them together to fight the challenges of America, while blacks were slaves, their culture and society taken from them, and their families broken apart. Considered inferior, they were kept on the lowest rungs of the social ladder.

This is how things persisted in this country for over three hundred years: Jews came here by choice, began a new life, and eventually entered American society; blacks, who were forced here against their will, were enslaved, then, after emancipation, were set apart, discriminated against, and often the target of lynchings, cross-burnings, and other brutalities and intimidations. But from Julius Rosenwald, the Sears, Roebuck founder who helped build schools for blacks throughout the South, to Joel Elias and Arthur Springarn, who helped found the NAACP, Jews offered what assistance they could.

Yet, with the overturn of *Plessy v. Ferguson* in 1954, a major movement for dramatic change in American history began to take shape. Whereas previous litigation had won blacks some minor victories, the Supreme Court's decision provoked major social and political change in American life. Little is recorded, however, about Esther Brown, the Jewish woman in Topeka, Kansas, who instigated the suit in the first place. Though Oliver Brown was the black plaintiff named in the case, it was a Jewish woman who had the same last name as Oliver who had initiated the challenge to the status quo. Esther Brown had no involvement with the black educational system other than to resent the fact that her black housekeeper's children were being educated in inferior schools. When a school bond came up for a vote, she protested the "separate but equal" dilapidated shack that passed as the black school house. Her white friends and neighbors were not pleased with her outburst. Hiring an attorney and raising funds for his fees, she tried to persuade the local NAACP to protest the bond, only to discover that it had no interest in arousing any possible antagonism.

Local black leaders hesitated out of fear that some black teachers would lose their jobs if the schools were desegregated. Over a period of years in which she actively pressed local school issues, Esther Brown was threatened and insulted, a cross was burned on her lawn, her husband was fired from his job, her father-in-law called her a Communist, and she suffered a miscarriage. The local NAACP secretary later said the task could hardly have been accomplished without her, although opposition to segregated schools had been in the air for years.[4]

When the NAACP's Legal Defense Fund (LDF) finally did bring a suit, it was headed by their lead attorney, Thurgood Marshall (who, in 1967, would become the first black member of the U.S. Supreme Court). But Jack Greenberg, his second in command, was one of many white lawyers involved in the earliest days of the LDF who were Jewish. Greenberg's involvement was fine: He was from the North. But for Southern Jews, *Brown* carried a basic philosophical problem:

> From the time of the prophet, who counseled the Jew to pray for the welfare of the land of which he is a part, until today, when in our prayerbooks we ask for God's blessing upon the rulers of our respective countries, the Jew has stood for loyalty to country and obedience to law. . . . However the problem of the Southern Jew today is in not knowing what constitutes the law. Good citizenship in the South today means adherence to local majority will rather than compliance with a Supreme Court decision which is considered a usurpation of power.[5]

Not only did *Brown* bring with it this Judaic problem of legal adherence, but it caused great concern for individual Jews who were trying so hard to assimilate and disappear into their local communities. As famed Southern writer Harry Golden explained: "While Protestants imposed a silence on their clergymen because they feared the Negro, Jews imposed a silence on their rabbis because they feared white Protestants."[6] Though Jews' liberal beliefs urged them to side with blacks, their own economic and social welfare called for them to keep their mouths shut and not rock the boat. As Rabbi Charles Mantinband of Hattiesburg. Mississippi used to relate, the position of Jews in the South could be objectified in a little ditty: "Come weal / Come woe / My status / Is quo."[7]

This attitude prevailed throughout the synagogues of the South, where Jews who wanted to assimilate feared they had the most to lose and where rabbis had to submit to a *sha-sha Yidden* ("quiet-quiet Jews") demeanor or find jobs elsewhere. Although a few Southern rabbis fought against discrimination—Perry E. Nussbaum in Jackson, Mississippi; Charles Mantinband in Hattiesburg, Mississippi; Alfred L. Goodman in Columbus, Georgia—by and large even Martin Luther King, Jr. admitted that he was disappointed by the lack of rabbinic response to civil rights: "It is surprising how seldom ministers and rabbis in the South or North have preached the truth of the biblical teaching on the brotherhood of man with courage and conviction."[8]

But this was not the case for Northern-based national Jewish organizations that railed against segregation and the Jim Crow perfidies perpetrated against blacks. As John Slawson, head of the American Jewish Committee, wrote in the *New York Times* in 1967:

> Jews for the most part are for civil rights, not to diminish Negro anti-Semitism, but because it is right and just and compellingly a necessity. We shall continue to pursue this course. We view Negro equality as a challenge calling for a moral commitment by all Americans of every race and religion.[9]

Despite Slawson's and other leaders' efforts, too often both Northern and Southern Jews felt that they had their own headaches and their own agendas. This was most acutely felt by Southern Jews who resented the holier-than-thou carpetbaggers from up North.

> The extreme right wing of the Jewish community and the great silent majority—dolefully searching for "middle ground"—agreed on one issue: the undesirability of northern Jewish interference in southern civil rights struggles. The southern Jews bitterly resented the meddling of the Union of American Hebrew Congregations [Reform Judaism's congregational organization], of the American Jewish Congress, and of the wild-eyed fanatics running B'nai B'rith's Anti-Defamation League (ADL), for these groups pretended to be speaking on *behalf* of southern Jews.[10]

Orthodox Jews also had limited interest in civil rights. As one Orthodox rabbi wrote, "Beleaguered as we are with problems related to Jewish survival, we cannot afford the luxury of dissipating our energies in a perpetual rush to nowhere."[11]

Essentially, the Orthodox Jewish attitude most often expressed was that of Rabbi Marvin Schick of Agudath Israel, an umbrella organization of ultra-Orthodox congregations and institutions:

> I do not advocate the active participation of the several major Orthodox organizations in the Civil Rights movement. The agenda of these groups is too crowded with unfinished business to permit the luxury of involvement in problems outside the periphery of Jewish life.[12]

Aiding the Orthodox poor and the Orthodox infirm, ensuring Orthodox religious education and Orthodox observance was their focus—not the plight of blacks.

In general, the Conservative community also refrained from being too involved with civil rights. Though the rabbinical community would send a few delegates from its conventions to aid King in his many campaigns, Conservative Jews had serious reservations about this. As the influential Conservative rabbi Arthur Hertzberg wrote at the time:

> The Negro is today fighting for his rights, and Jews, along with all other men of good will, must certainly stand beside him. But Jews are today also continuing to work at preserving and trying to define the meaning of their particular survival and identity, in the light of their own tradition and historic experience. Since this is a parochial concern of their own, they must here stand alone.
>
> Our age does not like aloneness; it seems to prefer togetherness on every level. But any serious Jewishness must live in tension between that which unites it with others even in the most moral of struggles and that which sets it uniquely apart.[13]

Mostly it was Reform Jews—rabbis and laity—and unaffiliated Jews who *did* respond to the call from blacks in the South. As Rabbi Arthur Lelyveld, who was seriously beaten by Southern racists during a civil rights campaign in Mississippi and who eventually headed the American Jewish Congress, declared:

> It does not diminish our dignity as Jews when we seek to achieve the precious ability to feel *empathy* with Negro bitterness and frustration. The command that we do so comes to us directly out of the Torah: *V'atem y'datem et nefesh hager*—"You should be able to know the *very being* of the stranger for you were strangers in the land of Egypt." And not only in Egypt 3,000 years ago: we were there yesterday![14]

But the major push came from the American Jewish Committee, the B'nai B'rith, the Union of American Hebrew Congregations and the Synagogue Council of America. Their chief agenda was to fight discrimination against Jews, but they also calculated that helping those at the bottom rungs of the American social ladder would improve Jews' ability to climb that ladder. As historian Hasnia Diner has written:

> [B]lacks provided American Jews with a mission in their new country, a special role which they believed they were uniquely suited to carry out. Their history of suffering, their centuries of exclusion from the mainstreams of national culture . . . had predisposed them to understand the real needs of a similarly situated group. It was important that someone serve as the middleman between the oppressor and the oppressed, and Jewish leaders eagerly moved into that position. In doing this they believed they were not only helping blacks, but at the same time serving the larger society, contributing to the good and welfare of all. This service might possibly bring in its wake certain benefits for American Jews. It would win them thanks and recognition for doing a crucial job which no one else would—or could—do. That, in turn, could be of immense help in stabilizing the social and political lot of Jews.[15]

And so, though the civil rights movement was born in churches and found its leaders among Southern Baptist ministers—and even though King expected to get his most enthusiastic white allies from fellow clergy (ministers and rabbis) who knew all too well the words of God and of the meaning of justice for all people—the Jews who would go to the civil rights barricades would primarily be the leaders of mainstream Jewish organizations, religiously unaffiliated students and lawyers, social activists, and ordinary people who felt some moral responsibility to help those in need. Even for those who would later portray Jewish involvement as primarily self-serving and not really deriving from Jewish teachings, it would be deceptive to deny the basic truth. As Jonathan Kaufman wrote in his history of black-Jewish relations, *Broken Alliance:*

> Looking back, it would be easy to see the Jewish response to civil rights as driven largely by self-interest wrapped perhaps in the cloak of idealism and altruism. Jews benefited enormously from the terrain shaped by the civil rights movement. Jews were the first to use anti-discrimination laws to gain access to restricted apartment buildings in large cities. The growing tide of tolerance left by the civil rights movement opened opportunities for Jews as well as for blacks in law firms, corporations, and universities. But to focus on self-interest as a motive was to miss the passion and excitement that enveloped Jews, like other whites, and like blacks, as the movement swept forward. The civil rights movement spoke to the Jewish head, but it also spoke to Jewish hearts.[16]

4

"Out of Zion Shall Go Forth the Law": King and the Jews

The relationship between Southern blacks and Jews in the time of Martin Luther King, Jr., was a unique divergence from the usual polarity of color and race in the U.S.: Though Jews, obviously, were white, they were deemed to somehow be different from other whites. As Jewish scholar Arnold Shankman writes:

> The Jew was the merchant who said "mister" [to blacks], the Northern philanthropist who built schools and hospitals [for blacks], the fellow sufferer in a society whose highest rungs were reserved for white Gentiles. The Jew was . . . the man on the make, the one who "has not lost faith in himself," the person to imitate. Though there were obstacles in the path of the Jew, Southern blacks were certain he would eventually rise to the top, and when he made it, it would somehow be easier for Negroes to advance.[1]

Though the relationship between blacks and Jews was somewhat different in the North, in the South they shared a common status.

Though Jews were white, Southerners saw them as outsiders—and as being above blacks socially, but not by much. As one black leader said, the name "Jew" in the South "always sounded like 'nigger' to me."[2]

Because of such sentiments, blacks and Jews shared certain bonds. Yet, despite this affinity, black churches in the South harbored a Christian skeleton in their closet: a two-thousand-year-old tradition of deicide. In his novel *Black Boy*, Richard Wright described this phenomenon:

> All of us black people who lived in the neighborhood hated Jews, not because they exploited us, but because we had been taught at home and in Sunday school that Jews were "Christ killers." With the Jew thus singled out for us, we made them fair game. . . . To hold an attitude of antagonism or distrust toward Jews was bred in us from childhood; it was not merely racial prejudice, it was a part of our cultural heritage.[3]

In an autobiographical sketch, Horace Mann Bond, the president of Lincoln University, traced how even the most educated of black people fell prey to this religious prejudice:

> Let me . . . [tell] you about something that happened to me in Atlanta, Georgia, in the Fall of 1916; I was then twelve years old.
>
> My family had but shortly before moved to Atlanta from the small Alabama town of Talladega; I had lived there, as before in similar settings, in the sheltered environment of a small Negro missionary college founded and operated in the New England Puritan tradition; in which tradition, indeed, both of my parents had received their college education.
>
> I was walking along a street near my house, and had to pass a small grocery store located in our neighborhood. There was a small boy—perhaps six years old—looking through the picket fence that surrounded the store. As I passed, he began to chant: "Nigger, Nigger, Nigger, Nigger." You may not believe it; but this was the first time I

could remember anyone calling me a "Nigger." And my response still surprises me; I retorted to the boy, "You Christ-killer!" And the little boy burst into tears, and I have felt badly about it ever since. . . .

I now think that, somehow, the word I used hung immanent in the Atlanta air; and, somehow, it had entered my mind, and remained there like a knife, waiting only for opportunity for release. But of course the thought that Christ had been killed, and by the Jews, and that this little boy was such a one, may have had a more ancient basis in my twelve-year old mind than I can now bring myself to admit.[4]

Despite this atmosphere, King developed his own philosophical and moral appreciation of the Jewish people. "Judaism," he said, "was always a religion that was part of everyday life. It seems to me that this demand for simplicity was a desire for high ethical character. . . . In other words, man . . . was to forever choose . . . the higher values."[5]

The prophetic Christianity of King's education focused on the ancient Hebrew prophets. And his association with such teachers as Reinhold Niebuhr, who was a militant cleric and ardent Zionist, further enhanced his affinity for Judaism and for the Jewish people. According to Horace Bond, Niebuhr "particularly wanted to have the Jewish people recognized for their genius in their culture, their religion, and their contribution to the history of mankind."[6] As Niebuhr wrote on this theme:

It is almost inevitable that we as Christians should claim uniqueness for our faith as a religion of redemption. But we must not claim moral superiority because of this uniqueness. For the efficacy of common grace and necessity of rational discrimination in all problems of justice do not give a religion of grace that practical superiority over a religion of law which we are inclined to assume. The fact that Jews have been rather more creative than Christians in establishing brotherhood with the Negro, and have done so particularly in a part of the country where the grace of a new life in Christ has been proclaimed in the experience of conversion in the sects of Protestantism, may prove that "saving grace" may be rather too individualistically conceived in Christianity to deal with collective evil. In short, if we measure the two faiths by their moral fruits, the Jewish faith does not fall short, particularly in collective moral achievement.[7]

Such lessons were not lost on King. In his early notes, he wrote that "Jesus was a Jew . . . [and] it is impossible to understand Jesus outside the race in which he was born. The Christian Church has tended to overlook its Judaic origins, but the fact is that Jesus of Nazareth was a Jew of Palestine. He shared the experiences of his fellow-countryman. So as we study Jesus we are wholly in a Jewish atmosphere."[8] And though the New Testament was the foundation of King's religion, it was the Old Testament, inflaming his spirit, that would ultimately lead the way to his lifelong calling. As Louis Baldwin noted about King's cultural and religious roots:

The Bible provided the model for King's prophetic role. His understanding of the prophetic posture largely resulted from his reading of Amos, Micah, Isaiah, Hosea, Jeremiah, and other Old Testament prophets in whose tradition Jesus and the Apostles stood. Although King spoke out of a twentieth-century American orientation, and especially out of the black experience, his words and actions were in many ways reminiscent of those of the Hebrew prophets.[9]

As King matured and recognized the foundations of his belief system he declared, "I draw not from Marxism or any other secular philosophy but from the prophets of Israel; from their passion for justice and cry for righteousness. The ethic of Judaism is integral to my Christian faith."[10]

Throughout his life, King sought to understand Jews and their outlook and stance toward the world. During a fundraising event at a Northern synagogue, he asked a rabbi about Jewish existence and persistence, about how the Jews had "maintained an unbroken historic consciousness, pride of heritage, and a faith in a God-appointed destiny."

"Dr. King," the rabbi answered, "from what source do you draw strength to climb the steep hill strewn with obstacles and danger?"

"You and I draw living waters from the same spring," King replied, "from the belief in a God of Love, Mercy and Justice. In the Jewish Prayer Book, I find words which express the essence of the Christian hope and promise: 'O may all, created in Thine image, recognize that they are brethren, so that, one in spirit and one in fellowship, they may be forever united before Thee. Then shall Thy kingdom be established on earth and the word of Thine ancient seer be fulfilled: The Lord will reign forever and ever.'"[11]

King also used the Jewish people as a reference point to reinforce his themes. As the guest speaker at the first American Jewish Congress convention held in a Southern state, Florida (and where blacks were allowed for the first time to stay at a Miami Beach hotel as guests who did not have to deal with any of the strictures of segregation), King stated in his address:

> Every Negro leader is keenly aware, from direct and personal experience, that the segregationists and racists make no fine distinctions between the Negro and the Jew. The irrational hatred motivating their actions is as readily turned against Catholic, Jew, Liberal and One-Worlder, as it is against the Negro. Some have jeered at Jews with Negroes; some have bombed the homes and churches of Negroes and in recent acts of inhuman barbarity, some have bombed your synagogues—indeed right here in Florida. As the Nazis murdered Catholic Poles and Jews, Protestant Norwegians and Jews, the racists of America fly blindly at both of us caring not at all which of us falls. Their aim is to maintain, through crude segregation, groups whose uses as scapegoats can facilitate their political and social rule over all people. Our common fight is against these deadly enemies of democracy. . . .

My people were brought to America in chains. Your people were driven here to escape the chains fashioned for them in Europe. Our unity is born of our common struggle for centuries, not only to rid ourselves of bondage, but to make oppression of any people by others an impossibility.[12]

King was also not loath to use the Holocaust as a reference point:

I have discussed the social effects of nonviolent mass direct action at length because I believe it is too often limited in its application merely to the civil rights movement. Perhaps if there had been a broader understanding of the uses of nonviolent direct action in Germany when Hitler was rising and consolidating his power, the brutal extermination of six million Jews and millions of other war dead might have been averted and Germany might never have become totalitarian. If Protestants and Catholics had engaged in nonviolent direct action and had made the oppression of the Jews their very own oppression and had come into the streets beside the Jew to scrub the sidewalks, and had Gentiles worn the stigmatizing yellow arm bands by the millions, a unique form of mass resistance to the Nazis might have developed.[13]

When it came to social involvement, political action, and a dedication to improving the standing of all people, King used Jews as role models. "Negroes," he admitted,

nurture as a persisting myth that the Jews of America attained social mobility and status because they had money. It is unwise to ignore the error for many reasons. . . . Jews progressed because they possessed a tradition of education combined with social and political action. The Jewish family enthroned education and sacrificed to get it. The result was far more than abstract learning. Uniting social action with educational competence, Jews became enormously effective in political life. . . . Nor was it only the rich who were involved in social and political action. Millions of Jews for half a century remained relatively poor, but they were far from passive in social and political areas. They lived in homes in which politics was a household word. They were deeply involved in radical parties, liberal parties and conservative parties— they formed many of them. Very few Jews sank into despair and escapism even when discrimination assailed the spirit and corroded initiative. Their life raft in the sea of discouragement was social action.

Without overlooking the towering differences between the Negro and Jewish experiences, the lesson of Jewish mass involvement in social and political action and education is worthy of emulation.[14]

King repeatedly used Jewish models. To African Americans who tried to make excuses for blacks' failures, he would exhort:

We must not use our oppression as an excuse for mediocrity and laziness. For history has proven that inner determination can often break through the outer shackles of circumstance. Take the Jews, for example, and the years they have been forced to walk through the long and desolate night of oppression. This did not keep them from rising up to plunge against cloud-filled nights of oppression, new and blazing stars of inspiration. Being a Jew did not keep Einstein from using his genius-packed mind to prove his theory of relativity.[15]

King also found a commonality between blacks and Jews as minorities:

There are Hitlers loose in America today, both in high and low places. As the tensions and bewilderment of economic problems become more severe, history's scapegoats—the Jews—will be joined by new scapegoats, the Negroes. The Hitlers will seek to divert people's minds and turn their frustrations and anger to the helpless and the outnumbered. Then whether the Negro and Jew shall live in peace will depend upon how firmly they resist, how effectively they reach the minds of the decent Americans to halt this deadly diversion.[16]

Throughout his career, in fact, King exhibited an appreciation for Jews not always shared by his own people and or by fellow

Christians. When, for example, Southern Baptist ministers tried to cast doubt on the validity of the Jewish faith, King responded firmly and passionately:

> I strongly disagree with the statement . . . that more than 5,500,000 Jews in America are "lost without hope." This type of narrow sectarianism can only lead to an irrational religious bigotry and serve to create a dangerous climate of separation between people of different religious persuasion.
>
> My theological position has always led me to believe that God reveals Himself in all of the great religions of the world and no religion has an absolute monopoly on truth.[17]

And so, King wrapping himself in a Judeo-Christian mantle, challenged the representatives of that heritage to join him in waging war against discrimination and injustice: "If we continue to worship at the pagan shrine of racism or totalitarianism of any color we shall never forge a stable, enduring, and just society. Our hearts and minds must be redirected to the hills where the hope and promise of a redeemed humanity was born. . . . In the words of the Prophet Isaiah (2:3): 'For out of Zion shall go forth the law, and the word of the Lord from Jerusalem.'"[18]

5

Montgomery:
The Journey Begins

On October 31, 1954, Martin Luther King, Jr.—young and vibrant and a speaker of formidable talent—became pastor of the Dexter Avenue Baptist Church in Montgomery, Alabama. Recently married in nearby Marion, he now occupied his first pulpit in which he did not have to defer to his father.

During these early years of his career, he met Joan Daves, the woman who would be his literary agent for the rest of his life. Daves was a German Jew born in 1919, whose father was killed in the Holocaust. She became associated with King in the early 1950s, shortly after starting her New York literary agency. Over the years, with her European contacts and ability, she developed a clientele of famous writers, including a few Nobel Prize winners. In addition to King, she represented Gabriela Mistral, Herman Hesse, Nelly Sachs, Heinrich Böll, and Elias Canetti.

Marie Rodell, Daves' partner, had made the original contact with King, but Daves was the one who wanted to meet the man she called the "extremely articulate, charismatic and visionary minister from the South."[1] Although they had a close personal relationship, Daves constantly complained to King that he was impossible to reach and that she found it difficult to adequately represent him. "Joan," King responded, "don't fire me." When King won his Nobel Prize in 1964, Daves went to Oslo with him.[2]

King came to Montgomery, then a town of almost 140,000 people—a third of them black—not anticipating the local dynamics of the white-black relationship. He was upset, as the historian Stephen Oates wrote in *Let the Trumpet Sound*, that

> there was not even a ministerial alliance to bring white and colored clergymen together. . . . It was clear why. White people wanted no contact on an equal basis with blacks. . . . Montgomery whites, of course, told themselves that "our niggers are happy and don't want integration." . . . They expected "niggers" to know their place and the mass of them to stay away from the polls and out of politics.
>
> To King's dismay, most local Negroes accepted all this with appalling apathy.[3]

Even Montgomery's black ministers were disorganized and were involved with their own parochial affairs, which did not include upsetting the status quo. King's only achievement during these early days in Montgomery was to become friends with the pastor of the First Baptist Church, Ralph Abernathy. The friendship would last for the rest of King's life.

The Jewish population in Montgomery was typical of that in many Southern communities. Most Jews tried to remain neutral and invisible on the issue of integration. Though they empathized with blacks, Jews feared for their social and economic well-being if they spoke out. Black leaders recognized this and assumed that the Jews "would succumb to fear and desert them in time of need."[4] Montgomery's Jews preferred to be so "invisible" that in the 1930s, during the infamous Scottsboro Boys case, which charged several young black men with the gang rape of a white woman, Benjamin Goldstein was fired as rabbi of Temple Beth Or when he protested the injustices of the trial. One rabbi remembered being an Army Air Corps chaplain in Montgomery during World War II:

> I spent eight months in Nashville, Tennessee, and eleven months in Montgomery, Alabama, and acquired an . . . intensive view of southern living. I found Nashville far more progressive and liberal in its attitudes than Montgomery. Although some of the Montgomery Jews we met had attended the better Ivy League colleges, I commented to my northern friends, "They hadn't had a thought since the Civil War."[5]

By and large, the situation of Jews in Montgomery was typical of the situation of Jews throughout the South: Jews were involved on both sides of the segregation issue. Some Jewish businessmen joined the racist White Citizens Council, maintaining that knowing the enemy from the inside was a good defensive move. And some Jewish women joined the Fellowship of the Concerned, a racially and religiously mixed organization that worked to peacefully implement integration.[6]

But overall, Montgomery's Jews found themselves in a difficult situation. Their defensiveness became especially obvious when the Montgomery bus boycott began on December 5, 1955, and Rabbi Maurice Eisendrath, the head of the Union of American Hebrew Congregations (UAHC), the national organization of Reform congregations, announced a pro-boycott position. It would be a Jew from Montgomery—Myron J. Rothschild, the president of Montgomery's Temple Beth Or—who would publicly chastise Eisendrath:

I am fully acquainted with the thinking of the vast majority of reformed [sic] Jewry in the Southeast and as such I do not hesitate to say to you that we do not wish an office of the Social Action Committee established in the South. We do not need it. Our thinking is so entirely different from yours, that we have come to the conclusion that we really do not need your advice. I will be charitable in my thinking and say that we think you simply do not understand the problems of the South.[7]

The response to Eisendrath was similar to what would happen when a Montgomery rabbi, Seymour Atlas, appeared in *Life* magazine during Brotherhood Week in 1956. A photo in which he was standing next to a black man created a furor in his temple. His temple's trustees demanded that Atlas persuade *Life* to print a retraction stating that Brotherhood Week had nothing to do with blacks.[8]

It didn't take Eisendrath long to respond to Myron Rothschild. Conceding his lack of familiarity with the South, he declared, "One did not have to live in Nazi Germany to be certain that our brethren were bestially butchered."[9] Chastising Rothschild for his "smug self-righteousness," Eisendrath stated. "Our fathers sought no such 'good will' at any price but rather pursued God's will at any cost, certainly of economic loss, ostracism, exile, and even death. If surrender to majority opinion had been the standard of Jewish practice, then we would not be discussing this matter as Jews today."[10]

Nevertheless, Eisendrath's views were not generally shared, not even among Southern rabbis. The consensus among Southern rabbis was aptly expressed by Rabbi William Malev:

I certainly agree that martyrdom is perhaps the noblest service which anyone can render to a great cause. My only contention is that no one has the right to martyr somebody else for the cause he believes in. Certainly, the Jews of the South have the sovereign and unalienable right to become martyrs in the cause of desegregation if they so wish.

I reject however any claim on the part of the national "defense" organizations to impose martyrdom upon the unwilling Jews of the South and to bask in their reflected glory of their self-sacrifice. It would seem to me that if they think so much of martyrdom they ought to come down South and try it for themselves.[11]

Even among Jewish lay leaders in the South, there was a feeling of

profound disquiet about the role of national Jewish organizations in the segregation conflict. In some Jewish communities—notably Montgomery and Selma—this attitude approaches paranoia. The villain of the piece, responsible for the actual and potential difficulties of Southern Jewry, is not the segregationist or the White Citizens Councils—but "Jewish agencies." Jewish lay leaders of the South, with few exceptions believe that the national Jewish organizations have coupled Jew and Negro in the public mind and thus have exposed small, weak Jewish communities to the implacable hatred which has been evoked by the battle over segregation. "You people are like Hitler," one such Southern Jew told a representative of a national Jewish organization. "You're stirring up anti-Semitism down here."[12]

While Jews debated about which course was best for them, 1956 brought changes in the life of Martin Luther King, Jr. He was arrested for the first time on January 26 for driving 30 miles per hour in a 25-mile speed zone and was represented by local attorney Morris Abram, who became another of King's close associates.

Morris Berthold Abram was born in 1918, three years after the lynching of Leo Frank in nearby Atlanta. (Frank was lynched by an antisemitic mob following his conviction for an alleged rape, a crime of which he was posthumously exonerated. The Frank lynching was another reason for the fear many Jews felt about their Southern status: They were afraid that at any moment they too could be the victims of a similar pogrom.) His father was a semi-illiterate immigrant from Romania, and his mother was the granddaughter of Elias Eppstein, one of the earliest Reform rabbis in the country. Her father had graduated from medical school in 1881 and put his sister through medical school, helping her to become one of the first female doctors in America. How did his mother, a woman of such an intellectual and cultural heritage, come to marry his father? "Well, the answer is quite simple," said Abram. "In that little town he was the best choice in a field of one."[13]

While a student at the University of Georgia, Abram was named head of a literary group. After asking President Franklin Delano Roosevelt in a letter to be an honorary member of the group, Abram was surprised to receive a letter of acceptance that also invited him to induct Roosevelt into the group at the Little White House in Warm Springs, Georgia. The elder Abram, the refugee from Romania, went with his son to the President's house. It was the crowning moment of his father's life.

Later awarded a Rhodes scholarship, Abram put his education on hold to serve in the military. While in military intelligence, he was promoted to major and was awarded the Legion of Merit. Immediately after the war, he served on the staff of Justice Robert Jackson at the Nuremberg trials. Growing up in a land of subtle (and not so subtle) anti-Semitism and then confronting at Nuremberg the perpetrators of the Nazi horrors, Abram came to understand "that when the veneer of civilization is cracked, even in the 20th century, the Jew is the first victim."[14] That conviction would be a driving force for the rest of his life.

After his term of service, Abram went to England to use his Rhodes scholarship. Returning to Georgia to practice law, he used the opportunity to also get involved with the burgeoning civil rights movement. "I'm a Constitutionalist," he said:

I don't think the Constitution can cover all aspects of human endeavor, but that makes no difference. If you don't have the Constitution, you will have human degradation. And therefore, when the Constitution says that all persons born or naturalized in the United States and subject to the jurisdiction thereof and of the state in which they reside, and that no state shall make or enforce any law abridging the privileges and immunities of a citizen of the United States, nor shall any state deny to any person within its jurisdiction, the equal protection of the law, that's what I believe and try to follow.[15]

In 1948, Abram began what would be a fourteen-year legal and political campaign against Georgia's county unit electoral system. This favored white voters in rural districts over urban voters from the more heavily black cities, sometimes by margins as great as one hundred to one. As a civil rights slogan, the phrase "one man, one vote" is sometimes attributed to Abram. In spite of repeated failures in lower courts, in 1963 he was a leading attorney in the Supreme Court ruling that "one man, one vote" was an indispensable principle of Constitutional law.

During the 1950s, through his involvement with the ADL, Abram worked on cases that would "unmask" the Ku Klux Klan. His efforts resulted in laws passed by fifty-three cities in five states. These laws hindered the activities of bigots who did not wish to be identified: though Klan members could meet and still have public functions, they could not be hooded. Their faces had to be bare for everyone to see. Before these laws, many of the most important members of various Southern towns had hidden their true identities under the white hoods of the Klan.

Abram went on to become the United States representative to the United Nations Commission on Human Rights, the first legal counsel to the Peace Corps, president of the American Jewish Committee, the president of Brandeis University, a candidate for the

Democratic senatorial nomination from New York, and head of UN Watch, a watchdog group that keeps an eye out for anti-Israel behavior in the United Nations. In the mid-1960s, he drafted international conventions designed to set standards on racial and religious discrimination around the world.

For his integrity, and reflecting his friendship with the King family, Daddy King recommended in 1983 that a Congressional committee approve Ronald Reagan's appointment of Abram to the federal Human Rights Commission. "I do not believe that many southern white people have had a longer experience in support of civil rights than Mr. Abram," said King, "[W]hatever he does on the commission, he will do on the basis of principle and conscience."[16]

Also during this time, King met the man who would be one of his most trusted advisers: Stanley Levison. A Jewish lawyer of independent means from New York, Levison would become King's friend, tax and business consultant, speechwriter, and most important fundraiser. As Andrew Young, the civil rights leader who would go on to be the mayor of Atlanta and ambassador to the United Nations, later remembered,

> Stan Levison was one of the first whites to offer help during the Montgomery bus boycott and was particularly key in national fundraising. He was introduced to Martin by Bayard Rustin, the first labor union supporter of the boycott, with whom we maintained a working relationship throughout the civil rights movement. By the time Stan became interested in the Southern civil rights movement, he had severed some of his ties to the old left, and was, I suppose, looking for a new cause to devote himself to. In helping Martin, there was much that he could do, for Martin knew nothing about fund-raising. Stan established a New York office for the boycott and created the first Montgomery Improvement Association mail-solicitation efforts.[17]

As the bus company and city fathers persisted in maintaining the segregationist status quo, the boycott by nearly 100 percent of the buses' black riders continued throughout the year. In November 1956—almost a full twelve months after the boycott began—the Supreme Court ruled that segregation on buses was unconstitutional.

Even so, when the buses were finally integrated in December, the overall Jewish response was not to rock the boat. Rabbi Eugene Blachschleger of Montgomery was typical when he said that he "made no public pronouncements on . . . [desegregation] either from my pulpit or in the columns of our daily press."[18] The lack of Jewish response did not go unnoticed. For many blacks, it spoke of the Jewish community's failure to step up to its divine calling. Horace Mann Bond wrote in 1965 that "much of the sharpest feeling among Negroes about Jews arises from a feeling that this man has especially let you down; he, of all men, ought to know what it was like; and how it had been."[19]

King didn't mince words regarding the support he and his cause received from national Jewish agencies—and the reverse attitude that was prevalent among the Jews of Montgomery:

> The national Jewish bodies have been most helpful, but the local Jewish leadership has been silent. . . . Montgomery Jews want to bury their heads and repeat that it is not a Jewish problem. I want to go on record and agree that it is not a Jewish problem, but it is a fight between the forces of justice and injustice. I want them to join with us on the side of justice.[20]

King's comment did not go unanswered. Rabbi William Malev responded with undisguised bitterness:

> Why does Dr. King single out the Jews in his accusation against their apparent silence and complacency? Why doesn't he accuse the Protestants or the Catholics of their reluctance to take sides with the Negro in this conflict?

The answer is obvious. There is a glaring inconsistency between the constant and vociferous speech-making on the part of the nation-al leaders of the "defense" organizations and the discreet and neces-sary silence on the part of the Jews whose position in the small towns of the deep South is far from enviable.

On the one hand, there is the constant beating of drums in Washington and New York by the national executives of our "defense" organizations, proclaiming the righteousness of the cause of desegregation, and, on the other, there are the Jews of the deep South, a very small minority, caught in the vise between the Negroes who demand that they side with them, and the white population who threaten them with violence if they do.... I agree with Dr. King that desegregation is not a Jewish problem. It is an American problem, and as such should be the concern of all Americans whatever be their creed or faith.[21]

Though one could claim that the response of Southern Jews to the boycott reflected the realities of their life in the South and the constraints (and sometimes also the fears) that they endured, it has to be admitted that there had been no universally positive response from Northern Jews, either. Rabbi Maurice Eisendrath ran into this situa-tion when he was forced to withdraw his invitation to King to be a guest speaker at the Union of American Hebrew Congregations' 45th General Assembly in Miami in November 1959. In his own address to the assembly, he furiously declared:

[B]ecause of our convening for the first time in this center contigu-ous to the deep South, I could not evade the stinging reminder that the sin of segregation—sin it is—is the monopoly of no region, for brotherhood is indivisible. What I have in mind, as I plunge once more into this heinous transgression of God's Fatherhood and man's all-inclusive brotherhood is the whole vast miasma of venomous racial hatred and segregation which rises like a stink in God's nostrils.[22]

True, some Southern Jews did believe in equality and a greater good as much as Eisendrath did, but they were dismissed by their peers as "firebrands" and gently pushed to the edge of acceptable society.[23]

King, however, didn't care about Jewish internecine politics. He had his own activities to worry about. In March 1957, he attended the independence day ceremonies of Ghana as a personal guest of Prime Minister Kwame Nkrumah. On May 17, 1957, together with Roy Wilkins of the NAACP and A. Philip Randolph of the Brotherhood of Sleeping Car Porters, the largest black union in the nation, he participated in the Prayer Pilgrimage for Freedom in Washington, D.C. In early August, he was named president of the newly formed SCLC. In February 1958, he began a voter registration campaign, the Crusade for Citizenship, and met with President Eisenhower. In September, his first book, *Stride Toward Freedom*, was published—and he was stabbed while on a book tour in New York. In 1959, he visited India, Jordan, Egypt, and Greece, and he participated in the second Youth March for Integrated Schools in Washington, D.C.

On November 29, 1959, King realized he could no longer be the pastor of the Dexter Avenue Baptist Church and keep all his activist commitments. As he had previously said, "Almost every week—having to make so many speeches, attend so many meetings, meet so many people, write so many articles, counsel with so many groups— I face the frustration of feeling that in the midst of so many things to do I am not doing anything well."[24]

So he left Dexter and in January 1960 was back in Atlanta as co-pastor of his father's Ebenezer Baptist Church.

6

A Refugee from the "Commercial Jungle": Stanley Levison

When Stanley Levison died in September 1979, Coretta Scott King called him "truly one of the great unsung heroes in the nonviolent struggle for justice and social decency in twentieth-century America. . . . Few people know of the magnitude of his contributions to the labor, civil rights, and peace movements."[1] Equally little known was the fact that he was Martin Luther King's most trusted white friend.

Born in 1912 in New York, Levison attended the University of Michigan and earned a law degree from St. John's University in 1939. Instead of practicing law, Levison invested in real estate and automobile dealerships and was soon quite wealthy. But his experiences during the Depression had also made him a radical. In the early 1950s, he supported Julius and Ethel Rosenberg during their trial for turning over nuclear secrets to the Russians, and he fought for those who were persecuted by the Smith Act (1940) or the McCarran Act (1950),

which punished anyone advocating subversive activities. These perse-
cuted included socialists, Nazis, Communists, and trade unionists.
When Joseph McCarthy began his witch-hunt for Communists,
Levison sided with the labor movement—and the Communist
Party—against the junior senator from Wisconsin. Levison's activities
soon attracted the attention of the FBI. Though no conclusive evi-
dence ever supported its contention, the FBI was convinced that
Levison managed money for the Communist Party in the United
States.

Among the "fellow travelers" whom Levison befriended was
Bayard Rustin, a highly educated black homosexual, conscientious
objector, and protégé of A. Philip Randolph, who headed the
Sleeping Car Porters union. Rustin was also close to Ella Jo Baker,
a former NAACP official, who fought with him against the McCarran Act.

Levison, Rustin, and Baker all shared a political radicalism that
was born from a hatred of racism. Since the Communist Party in the
1930s was the most active and outspoken of all organizations that were
seeking equality for all Americans, it was natural that the three of
them participated in party activities. But evidence suggests that only
Rustin joined the party itself. Levison never joined, but he was
marked by whatever remained of the party in the mid-1950s as someone who was sympathetic to it and whom its members could rely on
to raise funds for them or be their liaison to labor and civil rights
organizations.

By the mid-1950s, after the Soviet tanks rolled into Budapest and
suppressed democratic reforms in Hungary, the Communist Party lost
just about whatever was left of its appeal in the United States. Partly
to be as independent of the Party as possible, Baker, Levison, and
Rustin formed an organization called In Friendship, which raised
funds to combat racial discrimination. With Levison its liaison to the

American Jewish Congress, Rustin its titular head, and Baker its executive director, In Friendship began a fundraising campaign that would eventually lead to Alabama.

As Murray Friedman wrote in *What Went Wrong: The Creation and Collapse of the Black-Jewish Alliance:*

> The Levison-Rustin-Baker team was a remarkable alliance that bore little resemblance to the black-Jewish linkages of the past. Rustin was not accepted in the black middle-class establishment; nor was Levison, despite his American Jewish Congress connections, a part of the organized Jewish community. His Communist associations were known among civil rights insiders, and a number of Jewish civil rights activists, no doubt spurred by FBI warnings, kept their distance from him. Baker, a woman in King's heavily masculine world, felt even more strongly than her two partners that the leadership of the movement must come from below. (In time this conviction would bring her into conflict with King who, she came to feel, like Moses, seemed unaware that it was the movement that made him rather than the reverse.)[2]

When the movement in Montgomery began, Baker traveled there to witness the bus boycott and evaluate the situation. Soon Rustin was acknowledged as the first labor union supporter of the Montgomery Improvement Association, the coalition that was coordinating the boycott. Subsequently, Rustin introduced his friend Levison to King:

> Martin and Coretta were on their way to Baltimore, where King was to speak at an Omega Psi Phi fraternity convention banquet and receive their "Citizen of the Year Award." Bayard Rustin met him at the airport, and introduced three white friends who were with him. Harris and Clare Wofford were a young couple who had traveled to India and written a book on Gandhian nonviolence. . . . Rustin's third white companion [was] Stanley D. Levison. . . . Rustin had told both Wofford and Levison that he would like to secure funds for King to

travel to India and Africa, and they chatted about the possibilities as they drove to Baltimore.

After King had delivered his address ... King and his party headed back to Washington in the Woffords' car. Rustin and Levison told King that they and Baker had spent a recent evening discussing Rustin's idea of using the Montgomery movement as the basis for a wider civil rights initiative across the South. The attendance at the recent Institute on Nonviolence and Social Change clearly showed that other southern activists shared King's desire for more interaction, and with the Montgomery boycott complete, now was a propitious time for calling a southwide meeting. Levison and Rustin had drafted a memo detailing the merits and broader possibilities of a "Southern Leadership Conference on Transportation," and King agreed with their suggestions.[3]

From this suggestion, the SCLC was born.

Though most of its black members would know little about the Jew in New York who was working so hard to support their efforts, the irony in using "Christian" in the group's name was never really unveiled. Even an NAACP stalwart and King associate like the prominent lay leader of the Jewish Reform movement, Kivie Kaplan, would never know the facts. In 1962, Kaplan wrote to King:

I note that the name you have is SOUTHERN CHRISTIAN LEADERSHIP CONFERENCE. I certainly would be happy that you have some Jewish leadership as well as Christian and possibly change the name to SOUTHERN LEADERSHIP CONFERENCE because I know that we do have Jewish leaders who are fighting for justice along with the Christian leaders.[4]

In the meantime, In Friendship arranged for a concert in New York on December 5, 1956, starring Duke Ellington and Harry Belafonte, to raise funds for the Montgomery Improvement Association. Afterwards, Belafonte became another close adviser and friend to King.

Another fellow traveler recruited by In Friendship to help the Montgomery boycott was attorney Arthur Kinoy, who had grown up facing discrimination because he was Jewish. During his early days as a student at Harvard, he became decidedly leftist and joined the John Reed Society, named after the American journalist who traveled to Russia during the Bolshevik Revolution and became a Communist hero.

After becoming a lawyer, Kinoy focused on those on the bottom rung of American society; like Levison, he championed victims of the Smith Act and other forms of Red baiting. When Baker returned from Montgomery, she asked Kinoy to support the boycott. He leaped at the chance to have, as he put it, "a close relationship with an exploding new social force."[5]

In the meantime, the New York triumvirate—Baker, Rustin, and Levison—was persuading "King to launch a voter-registration campaign. . . . Ella Baker [went] to Atlanta to set up SCLC's office for the effort and to organize . . . rallies. Levison drafted a letter that went out over King's signature seeking to enlist the support of blacks and sympathetic whites in the registration drive. The campaign would not conflict with NAACP efforts, the letter made clear, but would instead implement the legal advances of that organization. The registration of black voters quickly gained momentum."[6]

Around this time, King and Levison became closer. King recognized that Levison was bluntly honest and wanted nothing from him other than to be of help, and theirs became a friendship that only death could bring to an end. Though King would offer Levison payment for the many activities he performed for him and the SCLC, Levison always refused. In a letter to King, he stated:

> My skills were acquired not only in a cloistered academic environment, but also in the commercial jungle where more violence in varied forms occurs daily than is found on many a battlefront. Although our culture approves, and even honors, these practices, to me they

were always abhorrent. Hence, I looked forward to the time when I could use these skills not for myself but for socially constructive ends. The liberation struggle is the most positive and rewarding area of work anyone could experience.[7]

Levison told King that he had been previously involved with members of the Communist Party and also about his other leftist activities. But that, he said, was all in the past and played no role in his present dedication to King and his civil rights struggles. When Levison said that he had never been a member of the Party, King took him at his word.[8]

But other players in the field of black-white relations had great doubts about King and his advisers. Resentful of King's success in Montgomery, his new stature, and the fact that funds that would have gone to them were now being directed elsewhere, they found it easy to portray King as an outsider who was being influenced by Communists. Especially with the leaders of In Friendship—all acknowledged fellow travelers—having such an influence on King's activities, this was an easy charge to make and to have stick. In addition to fundraising, Levison also became involved in King's literary efforts, negotiating and obtaining for him a book contract with Harper Brothers.

The book that resulted was *Stride Toward Freedom* (1958), an autobiographical account of the Montgomery action. Levison supervised the project, contributed sections (as did Rustin and Wofford), and did not hesitate to criticize King's writing. He told King that his account of the Montgomery protest sounded egotistical. There were also serious omissions and misinterpretations, Levison told him, concerning voting and registration, black self-improvement, and pursuit of social goals. With the final chapter unfinished and the deadline approaching, Levison, Rustin, and Wofford each drafted passages that were integrated into the published text.[9]

The In Friendship group, especially Levison, became more and more a part of King's life. Rustin became King's executive assistant, and Levison labored in the background as King's counsel, tax consultant, article- and speechwriter, and promoter of *Stride Toward Freedom*.[10]

By 1960, Levison was so trusted a friend that King spoke with him by phone every day: conferring, making plans, discussing life and religion—the Baptist talked to the very nonobservant Jew. "King would call Levison almost every night. Usually they discussed politics, but sometimes they argued about religion. It was inconceivable to King that a man as idealistic as Levison could have no belief in God. 'You believe in God, Stan,' he kidded Levison. 'You just don't know it.'"[11]

But Levison's closeness to King was not without its detractors. One of the first reactions of Harlem congressman Adam Clayton Powell, then one of the most powerful black members of Congress, when he was invited to become an SCLC board member was to condemn Levison for his influence over King.[12]

Though Rustin's and Baker's influence over King would wane, Levison remained a King insider to the very end. Never a sycophant, never trying to push his way to the forefront of King's attention, Levison would stay a trusted ally of the King family and of the older generation of civil rights leaders for years past King's death. Just before he died in 1979, Levison received the Martin Luther King Award from Atlanta's King Center for his efforts on behalf of the civil rights movement.

J. Edgar Hoover liked to believe that Levison was part of the Communist conspiracy to destroy the United States, and that through his influence over King he would create a revolutionary movement of disgruntled, maybe violent blacks who would stir up civil unrest. Others have claimed that the economic and social travails of the

Depression triggered a moral imperative in Levison to challenge injustice and fight for the rights of all men. Thought exactly what motivated Levison cannot be pinpointed with certainty, it can be said that even though he identified minimally as a Jew, he completely subscribed to Judaism's trademark concern with social justice.

7

"Moses" Returns to Atlanta

W hen Martin Luther King returned to Atlanta in 1960,
even the governor of Georgia, Ernest Vandiver, was moved to comment: "Wherever M.L. King, Jr. has been, there has followed in his
wake a wave of crimes including stabbings, bombings, and inciting of
riots, barratry, destruction of property and many others. For these reasons, he is not welcome in Georgia."[1]

The city that King returned to had the busiest airport in the
South and was home base to Coca-Cola. But it was thoroughly segregated. Though its white population was fairly enlightened (at least, in
contrast to those in the rest of the South), the majority of its blacks still
did menial work and faced "whites-only" restrictions wherever they
went.

Though Atlanta's Jews were more liberal than Jews in smaller
towns and cities of the South, they still shared a similar philosophy. As
the Southern Jewish journalist, Harry Golden, wrote in 1955,

> [T]he Southern Jewish proprietary class is inclined to be nervous
> about too liberal a concern with the Negro problem on the part of
> fellow Jews—they call it "rocking the boat." In the current Negro
> movement toward desegregation, they have maintained a strict neu-
> trality. They are too much exposed themselves, their attitude seems
> to be, to become "crusaders" for others. Though they will not say so
> openly, much of their argument for neutrality is based on the folklore
> that Gentile society must have its *kaporeh* (scapegoat), and that if the
> Southerners should lose their Negro *kaporeh,* they might very well
> look around for another.[2]

This was not an unwarranted position. In 1915, in Marietta,
Georgia, Leo Frank, the Jewish manager and co-owner of an Atlanta
pencil factory, had been lynched by a mob that was incited by racists
and anti-Semites. Frank had been the president of the B'nai B'rith
chapter in Atlanta. On April 27, 1913, the disfigured body of Mary
Phegan, a thirteen-year-old girl who worked in Frank's factory, was
found in its basement. Frank admitted that he had personally paid her
her wages the day before. After it was determined that no one had
seen her since, Frank was arrested for her murder. A few days later,
police took a black janitor who worked at the factory, Jim Conley, into
custody after he was seen washing blood off his shirt. The blood was
never tested, the shirt soon disappeared, and, a few weeks later,
Conley told the district attorney that he had seen Frank kill the girl.
Conley changed his statement three times, yet it was the basis of a
successful prosecution against Frank. The presiding judge sentenced
him to hang—and whites in Atlanta rejoiced.

After the Georgia Supreme Court and the U.S. Supreme Court
refused Frank's petitions for a new trial, Governor John Slaton com-
muted Frank's sentence to life imprisonment in June 1915. Out-
raged Georgians took the law into their own hands two months
later, when, in the middle of the night, they dragged Frank away from

his prison farm and hung him on a tree a few blocks from Mary Phegan's birthplace.[3]

But the times were different now than they had been in Leo Frank's day: The struggle for civil rights and equality was in the air. Atlanta was changing, mostly through the efforts of its established black leaders, who included Daddy King, and a city government that was fairly moderate and reasonable and was headed by Mayor William B. Hartsfield and Police Chief Herbert Jenkins. But everyone agreed that change would occur gradually. There would be no revolution in Atlanta.

"Our experience here meeting with blacks was very different from that of whites elsewhere in the South," said Sam Massell, who would succeed Ivan Allen as mayor in 1968. "We had the black academic center of the country here. We had blacks who were well read and world traveled. You'd sit down to a conference table, for example, look up, and notice that all the blacks in the room were wearing Phi Beta Kappa keys."

Street action was not the style of the postwar black power structure. Nor was it the style of—nor comprehensible to—Mayor Hartsfield and his chief of police, Herbert Jenkins, nor of the key members of the business elite like Robert Woodruff, the chairman of the Coca-Cola Corporation; Ivan Allen, Jr., the president of the Ivan Allen Company; Mills B. Lane, Jr., the president of Citizens & Southern Bank; and Dick Rich and Frank Neely of Rich's. The black leaders cultivated, instead of a mass movement, a few key political liaisons; they made themselves known to Mayor Hartsfield and felt encouraged, by his civil reception when they called upon him, to continue to take their proposals and recommendations directly to the top. Thus, most of Atlanta's early civil rights accomplishments—the integration of the police force, the integration of the buses, the integration of the school board, the integration of the public golf courses, and eventually, in the most delicate and brilliant of the contrived scenes, the introduction of a handful of black students into a white high school—were handled sagely, with deft coordination, by men speaking in soft voices, wearing summer suits, and behaving with almost exaggerated politeness. The necessary public actions—a touch of civil disobedience here, some arrests there—were secretly choreographed beforehand by the mayor, the black business leaders and ministers, the white business elite, and the white chief of police.[4]

An example of how well the city government and black leaders worked together was the desegregation of Atlanta's transit system.

"On January 9, 1957," wrote Jenkins, . . . "a group of Negro ministers boarded a bus in downtown Atlanta and sat in the 'white only' section of the bus. The driver left his route immediately and drove the bus back to the garage, whereupon the Negroes got off and departed.... [Soon] Mayor Hartsfield was on the phone in one of his 'jumping up and down calls.'" The mayor was taken by surprise by the black ministers, who'd made their startling step in response to the pressure they'd felt emanating from King and Montgomery, and from hundreds of black students growing restive at the Atlanta University Center.

After calling a meeting of white business leaders, transit company officials, and the black power structure, Hartsfield proposed that a lawsuit be filed attacking Georgia's segregation law for municipal conveyances. To file a lawsuit, plaintiffs would be required. Jenkins was assigned the task of locating individuals willing to violate the law and make a test case. "I telephoned the Rev. William Holmes Borders, leader of the ministerial group, and asked him if he would mind being arrested," wrote Jenkins. "The Rev. Mr. Borders, a man of wide intelligence and vast understanding, replied that he was not happy at the prospect and would have some difficulty explaining it to his congregation. Then he asked me exactly what I had in mind."

Together they planned the time and place that black leaders would again board a bus, be led off by Atlanta police, and be driven away in the paddy wagon. "In due course," wrote Jenkins, "the federal court held the segregated seating law to be null and void and the city's transportation system was desegregated peaceably. . . . The whole community had won uninterrupted transportation service, for there took place no boycotts as in Montgomery."[5]

As for Atlanta's Jewish community, if cultural assimilation was the basic attitude of post–World War II Jewry, then Southern Jews were the most adept in the whole country at practicing it. They were better off financially, better educated, concentrated in higher socioeconomic groups, and more urban than non-Jews. Nevertheless, they were not entirely secure and, regardless of where they lived, they shunned controversy since one of their region's cardinal virtues was conformity. Yet, Atlanta was perhaps the most cosmopolitan of Southern cities, and some Jews there were ardent advocates of integration. One of them was Dr. Marvin C. Goldstein, a World War II veteran who had returned from overseas to open a dental practice.

> Integrated doctors' offices were . . . uncommon in 1950s Atlanta. Blacks seeking treatment would have to enter in the rear, avoiding white patients in the waiting room.
>
> "I decided that everyone would be treated equally," Dr. Goldstein [said] . . . "Several patients were not happy and I indicated they had the right to go somewhere else."
>
> After integrating his practice, Dr. Goldstein earned a reputation as a dentist to the civil rights movement. "I treated Dr. King's children, and the Rev. [Ralph David] Abernathy's."[6]

But by and large, Atlanta's Jews knew their place in the Southern scheme of things. They may have accumulated wealth and climbed up the social ladder, but no matter how well they did—socially, politically, professionally—as Jews, they were still considered outsiders.

When it came to civil rights, the various movements of Atlanta Jewry found their rabbis reflecting their congregations' attitudes. Yet, Harry H. Epstein, who was Orthodox, had a pulpit at a Conservative congregation, Ahavath Achim, and had been involved with black issues as far back as 1948. Epstein spoke to many audiences—black and white, Jewish and Christian—about the inherent injustice of segregation, and he backed *Brown v. Board of Education* when it became the law of the land. Over the years, he publicly and repeatedly defended King's efforts to free blacks from second-class citizenship. But since Epstein had to adhere to the priorities and the preferences of his congregation, he was never a major player in Atlanta white-black relations.[7]

On the other hand, Jacob M. Rothschild, the rabbi of the Reform Hebrew Benevolent Congregation (which was better known as The Temple), was the most influential of the group. From his first arrival in Atlanta in 1946, he never relaxed his attack on the subjugation of blacks. In a Yom Kippur sermon delivered in October 1948, years before civil rights had a national audience, Rothschild expressed his shame at "the growing race hatred that threatens the South" and called for his people to "be among those who are willing to do something" to reverse the tide.[8]

Unlike other Southern rabbis, Rothschild was fortunate: he had a congregation that supported him. "When one member of his congregation resigned from the temple because she was incensed at seeing Rothschild's daughter with a Negro friend in a restaurant, the [synagogue's] Board of Trustees wrote her a letter regretting that she had failed to "learn the lesson of Judaism taught by our rabbi in word and deed."[9]

When the *Brown v. Board of Education* decision was announced in 1954, Rothschild declared in a sermon to his congregation:

It has become a commonplace to state that no one living in the North can truly understand the frenzy roused in the South by [the] recent decision of the Supreme Court. . . . [O]ne must understand that hysteria prevails, that there has been an abdication not alone of reasonableness, but of reason itself, to appreciate the climate of today's South. Basic democratic freedoms no longer exist. There is no freedom of thought or speech; government is rapidly becoming government not by law but by men. It is in such an atmosphere that the Jew finds himself. If white Christians are fearful, the Jew is panic-stricken. He sees himself as another minority, the next potential victim of the mass hysteria. Nor does it prove effective to point out that from sheer practical considerations, leaving out all calls to noble vision and high ideals, he would do better to defend the principles of democracy. He prefers to take on the protective coloration of his environment, to hide his head in the cotton patch in the dual hope that he won't be noticed and the problem will go away.[10]

Rothschild's son, Bill, recalls his father's attitude: "We were listening to the radio . . . and [s]ome local civic leader was saying the public schools ought to remain open and we ought to obey the law because it would be good for business, and Dad kind of looked at me and sort of half looked out the front windshield and said, 'Why don't they do it because it's right?' "[11]

As part of his commitment not only to black-white relations but to the entire Atlanta community, Rothschild created a support group with Christian clergy leaders who shared his contempt for segregation. This led Rothschild to participate in vociferous public stands against the segregationist actions of Governor Orville Faubus of Arkansas. This was one of the first attempts by clerics in the South to stake out a position of humanity and justice for all people.

In the fall of 1957, white mobs rioted outside Central High School in Little Rock, Arkansas, as nine black students tried to enroll. Governor Faubus warned that "blood [would] run in the streets" if the school was integrated, and he called out the National Guard to protect against the black students' entry. In reaction, eighty Atlanta Christian clergymen released a statement, the first of its kind in the South, which appeared in the Atlanta Constitution and came to be known as the Ministers' Manifesto. It read, in part: "Freedom of Speech must at all costs be preserved. . . . As Americans and as Christians we have an obligation to obey the Law....The Public School System must not be destroyed ... [and] hatred and scorn for those of another race.... can never be justified."

Rothschild [who had sat in on the planning and drafting of the manifesto, but did not sign it because it was too explicitly Christian] honored the courage of the ministers in a sermon and in a newspaper article . . . , "Eighty Who Dared: A Salute to My Christian Colleagues": "Inevitably ministers who confront the mores of their day with the timeless morality of their religious faith find themselves at best unpopular and frequently reviled and threatened. How could it be otherwise? If their people were in agreement with them, it would hardly be necessary for them to speak out at all."[12]

To this day, some people say that Rothschild's outspokenness provoked the bombing of The Temple on October 12, 1958, which caused great damage. But even the bombing did not stop him from speaking out:

[He] began seminars to help prepare his people for ... desegregation. In 1958, chiding his fellow-members of Rotary, he advised them that the Negro had every right to be impatient with a white community unreceptive to racial progress. At the mayor's request, Rothschild gave the key speech to a meeting of hotel and restaurant owners during a time when the public accommodations issue was especially urgent. In 1961, he was one of the founders of, and speakers for, a group created to prepare the community for school integration; it was called HOPE (Help Our Public Education). In short, Rabbi Rothschild was involved in practically every civil rights issue in Atlanta.[13]

King arrived in Atlanta in the middle of this situation. Because Daddy King was an influential member of the community, his son decided not to participate in any local activities that would upset that standing.

In the meantime, the Rothschilds brought King into their hearts and home:

A dinner party at the Rothschild's home was arranged: the Rothschilds invited Martin and Coretta King, Joe and Betty Haas, Cecil and
Hermie Alexander, and Hermie's mother, Rosetta Weil, visiting from
New Orleans. [As Rothschild's wife later recalled], "The Kings arrived
... much later than the others.... No explanation was necessary. But
Martin apologized anyhow and explained that they has been delayed
trying to find our house.... They finally had to drive up to one of the
other houses to inquire. As Martin told us this, he quickly added, 'But
we were careful not to embarrass you with your neighbors. I let
Coretta go to the door so they'd think we were just coming to
serve a party.' "[14]

But King's fame soon brought him to the forefront of the civil
rights movement in Atlanta. In Greensboro, North Carolina, black
students from North Carolina Agriculture & Technical College sat at
a segregated lunch counter in a Woolworth's store and asked to be
served. As college students across the South began their own sit-ins,
King urged them on, declaring their actions "one of the most significant developments in the civil rights struggle."[15] Soon, he was asked
for more than just his support.

After a conference in April 1960 at Shaw University in Raleigh,
North Carolina, King urged the college students who were present to
form an organization that would be a youthful branch of the SCLC.
Instead, the students formed their own independent group, SNCC,
that would organize their sit-ins and demonstrations.

Months later, SNCC members in Atlanta asked King to join
them at a sit-in at Rich's department store.

The store's Jewish owner, Dick Rich, was in the same quandary
faced by many Jewish merchants in the South: If he desegregated his
store, he would lose many of his white clients; if he didn't, he would
lose many of his black ones. In fact, he lost many of both.

After King was arrested for trespassing at Rich's, he refused bail and was sentenced to prison. Mayor Hartsfield soon arranged to have King and the students who were arrested along with him released. But King was not set free. He had been arrested months earlier in DeKalb County for driving with an out-of-state license, and his actions at Rich's had constituted a violation of his parole. Despite efforts to keep him out of DeKalb's Klan territory, King was removed from Atlanta and sent to Reidsville prison — one of the most dismal prisons of the South. Coretta cried in fear for her husband's life.

King's release from Reidsville became one of those pivotal events that literally changed the course of history. On October 28, 1960, King left Reidsville. All it had taken was the conniving of Mayor Hartsfield and the influence of a presidential candidate, John F. Kennedy. It also involved attorney Morris Abram and Harris Wofford, who was now an aide to Kennedy.

At the time of King's incarceration, Abram had been a long-time friend of Daddy King, whom he considered one of finest men he had ever encountered. In fact, he would tease Martin by saying that had it not been for his father, Martin would be a nobody. King would always concede Abram's point.[16]

As it happened, Wofford called Abram to find out about King's status:

"Atlanta's supposed to be the enlightened leader of a New South, Hartsfield's the best mayor in the country, and you're a lawyer who can do anything. So why is Martin still in jail?" Morris said that it was fortuitous I had called; he was leaving for a meeting at City Hall with Mayor Hartsfield and a group of Negro leaders. He would tell Hartsfield of my call and they would see what they could do. Senator Kennedy did not know of my call, I emphasized, but I knew he would appreciate a satisfactory resolution, with King's release from jail as soon as possible.[17]

Abram soon called Wofford back to tell him that Hartsfield had announced that presidential candidate Kennedy had personally intervened to secure the release of King. (Hartsfield needed someone to blame for something he couldn't overtly do himself.) Wofford went wild. Kennedy knew nothing about this, and would surely "hang" Wofford when the news reached him. With the campaign as close as it was, any hint of helping blacks could cost him the Southern vote.

But Kennedy issued a public statement, which, while not hanging King and Hartsfield out to dry, did not exactly offer anything that Republicans could use against him in the South. The matter became stickier, though, when King was transferred to Reidsville.

Coretta, five months pregnant, was convinced that her husband was in serious trouble in Reidsville. Not only was he sentenced to six months of hard labor, but Reidsville was not exactly a Negro-friendly environment. After Daddy King had asked Abram to help his son, Sargent Shriver, a Kennedy brother-in-law, was contacted by Wofford and asked to persuade Kennedy to call Coretta and offer some words of consolation. As Coretta King wrote in her autobiography:

> Daddy King was thinking in terms of practical things—of finding lawyers who could get Martin out of jail. He asked me to go with him to see … Morris Abram, who had become a friend of ours during our struggle and who had been very helpful with civil-rights cases.
>
> As I was getting dressed to go to see Mr. Abram, the telephone rang. The person at the other end said, "May I speak to Mrs. Martin Luther King, Jr.? Just a minute, Mrs. King, for Senator Kennedy."[18]

That humane call helped earn Kennedy his presidency. A confirmed Republican, Daddy King had already announced his support for Richard Nixon. But by calling Mrs. King, Abram was able to get King, Sr., to announce that because of Kennedy's demonstrated humanity and concern, he would not be averse to voting for the

Massachusetts senator. (Though Nixon had also been asked for assistance throughout Martin's ordeal, he offered none.) A subsequent call by Bobby Kennedy, the new U.S. Attorney General, to Oscar Mitchell, the judge who had sent King to Reidsville, soon achieved Martin's release. Daddy King's announcement about changing his vote has been credited with getting John Kennedy enough black votes to win the 1960 presidential election.[19]

By April 1961, King was back at work in the civil rights movement. He had already visited President Kennedy at the White House and was about to face a new phenomenon that would test the young president's commitment to civil rights: the Freedom Rides.

8

"Only Rabble-Rousers Recite Psalms with Negroes"

Of the many rabbis who came in and out of Martin Luther King's life, few would be as dedicated and colorful as Rabbi Israel Dresner. Dresner never dreamed that one day he would be locked up in several Southern jails, a whipping boy for segregationists, and the star of a Supreme Court case, *Dresner v. Tallahassee*. But his fire had been lit at an early age, and this *brenn* (someone who burns from within) never let it go out. "In those days," he remembered, "Jews were liberals. Not all, but most. Jews were not as wealthy, as suburbanized, as assimilated . . . [as they are now]. I was the son of immigrants, typical Jews, [and was] born on [Manhattan's] Lower East Side in a tenement building, not even in a hospital. It was not unusual for somebody [from that neighborhood] to be a person of the left."[1]

Dresner attended the University of Chicago and received ordination from what is now the New York School of the Hebrew Union College-Jewish Institute of Religion. In 1948, he was arrested for the first time in his life outside the British Commonwealth Building in New York for protesting British immigration policies in Palestine. He subsequently spent time in Israel as a kibbutznik. About twelve years later, after exhorting teens in his synagogue—Temple Sharey Shalom in Springfield, New Jersey—to personify the Jewish spirit of giving and commitment to fellow humans, he decided to practice what he was preaching and told his temple's leaders that he was going to join the Freedom Riders.[2]

The Freedom Rides had begun in May 1961 under the auspices of CORE, which was headed by James Farmer from then until 1966. Since 1946, the Supreme Court had barred segregation in interstate-regulated vehicles and facilities. But all the states of the Deep South flouted that ruling and had separate facilities for whites and blacks at bus stations. CORE, which wanted to publicize such practices, organized groups of volunteers to ride South and try to integrate those facilities. When King was asked to participate in the campaign, he told his staff, "CORE started the Freedom Ride and should get the credit. We will play a supportive role."[3]

In the meantime, the Reform movement's Union of American Hebrew Congregations had urged its membership to get involved: "It is essential that there be direct Jewish religious participation in the bus rides."[4] Subsequently, "nearly two-thirds of all white Freedom Riders were Jewish."[5]

Perhaps part of the reason for Jewish participation was acceptance of what King had said years earlier:

> [T]he segregationist makes no fine distinctions between the Negro and Jew. The racists of America fly blindly at both of us, caring not at all which of us falls. Their aim is to maintain, through crude segregation, groups whose uses as scapegoats can facilitate their political and social rule over all people.

> Our common fight is against these deadly enemies of democ-
> racy, and our glory is that we are chosen to prove that courage is a
> characteristic of oppressed people, however cynically and brutally
> they are denied full equality and freedom.[6]

When the first riders reached Alabama, one of the buses they were in was fire-bombed outside of Anniston. In Birmingham, Freedom Riders were beaten while police watched. On May 20, a bus entering Montgomery was attacked by a crowd wielding clubs and pipes. King wanted to get to the scene to lend assistance, but he was trapped in Ralph Abernathy's church as it was attacked by rocks and tear gas.

Over the course of the summer, hundreds of Freedom Riders were beaten, battered, and arrested. Israel Dresner was one of them. "If I am a Jew," he said, "I believe what the Bible tells me, and it tells me that 'God formed man of the dust of the ground, and breathed into his nostrils the breath of life; and man became a living soul.' He didn't seem to have been concerned with making differences between white and black and yellow."[7]

In June, the Interfaith Clergy Freedom Ride brought together four rabbis and fourteen ministers. It was organized by Rabbi Martin Freedman of Barnert Memorial Temple in Paterson, New Jersey, who was joined by co-religionist rabbis Israel Dresner, Walter Plaut, and Richard Hirsch:

> We boarded a bus in Washington D.C. [on June 14] and were sup-
> posed to be integrating facilities all along the way: Virginia, North
> Carolina, South Carolina, Georgia. There were ten white ministers,
> four black ministers and four rabbis. There were no Catholics [on the
> bus] . . . because the discipline of the church was much greater in
> those days; nobody could do anything without permission. We elect-
> ed one of the black ministers as the leader of the group, but he would
> back down every time there was a confrontation. This caused so

much dissension in the group that Plaut and Hirsch left and returned home, as did eight of the Protestant ministers.[8]

When the remaining group arrived in Sumter, South Carolina, the local sheriff made it clear he did not appreciate their presence and booted them out of town. At their final port of call—Tallahassee, Florida—little did they realize that they were about to begin a new trip, one that would take them three years to complete. Ready to fly home after their bus odyssey, they attempted to get service at the airport restaurant, but no one would wait on a racially mixed group. So they sat the counter all day and all night until the facility closed at midnight. After sleeping at a local Negro church, they returned to the restaurant at 7 A.M. and once again waited. They resolved not to eat anything until all of them had been served. They sat hungry.

The city police were soon called. A town clerk read them an ordinance demanding that they disperse. After failing to do so, they were arrested and charged with unlawful assembly. Pleading not guilty, the ten clerics were jailed when they refused to post bail.[9]

The Tallahassee Ten as they came to be known, were two rabbis—Dresner and Freedman—and Rev. Petty D. McKinney from Nyack, New York; Revs. Robert J. Stone, A. McArven Warner, and Ralph Lord Ray, from New York City; Rev. Arthur L. Hardge from New Britain, Connecticut; Rev. Wayne Hartmire, Jr., from Culver City, California; Dr. Robert McAfee Brown from Stanford, California; and Rev. John W. P. Collier from Newark, New Jersey.

In prison, other inmates tried to set Rabbi Freedman's bed on fire. The only Tallahassee clergyman to visit the jailed ministers was the local rabbi. To Dresner, the rabbi seemed terrified that the Freedom Riding rabbis might jeopardize the local Jewish community.

After being in prison for twenty hours, the group was finally arraigned, but in secret. At the trial, when Freedman was asked about his various "antisocial" activities, he stated that he was Paterson, New Jersey's, police chaplain. Dresner tried to sit with the black ministers who were also on trial, but was dragged away by police, who insisted on maintaining complete segregation, even in the courtroom.[10]

Eventually, the Freedom Rider case was heard before the Supreme Court, but Dresner v. Tallahassee took years to reach the court. In the meantime, Dresner was free while his appeal was pending. In an interview, he told a reporter that the racial situation in the South was comparable to the situation in Germany in the 1930s, when other nations considered Hitler's Jewish policies to be purely "internal matters." "Yet," Dresner said, "had someone—an outsider—interfered, there would not be six million dead." The comparison was one of relative evil, "but what is happening in the South is nonetheless evil within the American and Judaic tradition."[11]

For Dresner, the events in Tallahassee were a precursor of further adventures. Little more than a year later, in August 1962, King asked two Tallahassee alumni, Rev. Ralph Lord Roy and Dresner, to organize a group of clerics that would assault segregation in Albany, Georgia. This was Dresner's first meeting with King. He sat "next to King . . . and we sang a song, 'John the Baptist was a Baptist.' . . . Not too much later, some twenty of us were in this house and found ourselves surrounded by a White Citizens Council group. I was very scared. King was cool as a cucumber. He was just wonderful."[12]

As seventy-five visiting clergymen prayed and sang hymns outside Albany's city hall, police chief Laurie Pritchett pleaded with them leave. "I have no desire to put you in jail," he said. "Go about your normal way of life. Go in the name of decency. You have had your prayer. Go now."

Then, when he saw that the ministers would not move, as five hundred whites cheered and applauded, he said, "You have made your presence known by all news media. By your presence here, it is plain to see that you have come to aid and abet law violators." And he arrested all of them.[13]

To the charge of being a rabble-rouser and an outside agitator, Dresner declared, "I am an American, and these things are happening in America. What takes place in Georgia concerns me . . . as an insider. And what rabble-rousing is there in reciting psalms in public with Negroes? Aren't there some things that people of all races can do together without censure?"[14]

Of his time in Albany and the response of the Jewish community to what transpired there, Dresner would comment:

> Either we're men and equal American citizens, or we're not. . . . This fight by Jews against segregation in the South has made some of the tribes of Israel trembling tribes. We've been advised by this group and that group to be quiet, and not to become involved. But I believe that Jews must be supersensitive to bigotry and segregation because wherever democracy is flaunted the Jew is in danger. Democracy is the Jew's best defense.[15]

As Dresner's fame spread, he was asked to speak at more and more functions. And in January 1963, he was invited to attend the National Conference on Religion and Race in Chicago, which was sponsored by the National Catholic Welfare Conference, the National Council of Churches of Christ, and the Synagogue Council of America.

In July 1963, police clubbed him while he was participating in a sit-in that was protesting segregation in the building trades union at a construction site in Newark. It was ironic that he had survived so many hazardous situations in the South only to be injured in his home state. When asked if his activities would foster anti-Semitism, he said:

> Any bigot who hates a Negro for being a Negro hates a Jew anyway. . . . And when clergymen stand together, regardless of race or religion,

it makes it hard for a man to single out any one person for abuse. This kind of interfaith work has increased cooperation between clergymen everywhere, and it's far better and more meaningful than a "Brotherhood Week" celebration.[16]

In the summer of 1964, *Dresner v. Tallahassee* finally reached the Supreme Court. In its ineffable wisdom, the high court deemed the case a local issue and bounced it back to the Florida lower courts.

Refusing to post bond, nine of the original ten returned to Tallahassee, where they were again incarcerated. While in jail, they received a telegram from King:

> You are the valient [sic] ones. All America went to jail with you. Our spiritual limitations are shown by your physical incarceration. Your willingness to suffer, to go to jail without bond or paying of fines, is telling the truth about us. The nation's position is exposed. Our law is reduced to using technicalities to torture the testers of law. America's shame at this hour is expressed by its treatment of you who serve in Tallahassee. Your heroism is the nonviolent movement's moral witness to a world that has seen too little of the spirit and purpose of the prophets and disciples. Today it is your valient [sic] act that touches the conscience of Americans of good will. Your example is a judgement and an inspiration to each of us.[17]

By September 1964, Dresner joined ten thousand people in Washington who were protesting the plight of Soviet Jews in the USSR. About five hundred had come from New Jersey, including the contingent of twenty-two people from Dresner's temple. King sent a telegram to the event voicing his support.[18]

On April 24, 1966, King spoke at Dresner's temple. He condemned the three basic evils in society—racial injustice, poverty, and war—and was especially critical of the war in Vietnam. A year later, King was with Dresner again, this time at an anti-war event at New

York's Cathedral of St. John the Divine. Dresner left for a year-long sabbatical in Israel in July 1967. On April 5, 1968, he was awakened by a 5 A.M. phone call from Kol Yisroel, the Israeli radio station, asking him to comment on the assassination of Martin Luther King.[19]

In Dresner's library in Wayne, New Jersey, sits a book by King: *Why We Can't Wait.* On the flyleaf are these words, written in 1964: "To my dear friend Sy Dresner, 'With warm personal regards and deep appreciation for all that you are doing to make justice a reality.' Martin."

9

"Raging" Bull:
Hell in Birmingham

Martin Luther King called Birmingham "the most segregated city in America." The city was a Deep South bastion of intolerance and violence that considered lynchings and castration part of the logical and God-given right of whites to keep blacks in their place. Since 1956, Rev. Fred Shuttlesworth, the local SCLC affiliate head, had fought bigotry in Birmingham. He had the battle scars to show for his efforts: His home was bombed, both he and his wife had been assaulted (he'd been whipped; she'd been stabbed), and he had a long rap sheet at the local police station. But it wasn't until 1963 that King brought his special commitment to Birmingham, Alabama, and history was made.

In January, King had addressed the National Conference of Religion and Race in Chicago and declared that:

Two segregated souls never meet in God. Segregation denies the sacredness of human personality. Deeply rooted in our religious heritage is a conviction that every man is an heir to a legacy of dignity and worth. . . . Our Judeo-Christian tradition refers to this inherited dignity of man in the Biblical term the image of God. The image of God is universally shared in equal portions by all men. The tragedy of segregation is that it treats all men as means rather than ends and thereby reduces them to things rather than persons.

The Churches and Synagogues have an opportunity and a duty to lift up their voices like a trumpet and declare unto the people the immorality of segregation. We must affirm that every human life is a reflex of divinity, and every act of injustice mars and defaces the image of God in man.[1]

The "image of God" he faced in Birmingham was Eugene "Bull" Connor, the city's police commissioner.

Birmingham was then an industrialized home to almost 630,000 people. This included less than 4,000 Jews. Most belonged to Birmingham's Orthodox synagogue, Congregation Knesseth Israel, or its Conservative synagogue, Temple Beth El, or its Reform congregation, Temple Emanu-El. Jews in Birmingham were in the position common to most Jews throughout the South:

[I]n Birmingham there were "merchants" and "businessmen" . . . "[B]usinessmen" were part of the power structure and . . . "merchants" were not. The businessmen controlled the banks, primary industry, and utilities. The merchants controlled the stores. Businessmen were Gentiles; merchants were largely Jews. The first thrust of the Negro struggle had necessarily been directed against the merchants. The initial demands of the Negro groups involved unrestricted use of lunch counters and fitting rooms as well as better employment opportunities in the stores. No matter how much the merchants wanted to give in (and this varied greatly with the individual merchant), they could move no farther nor faster than the business and political power structures would permit. One of the roots of Negro anti-Semitism in the South consists of the fact that their initial struggle has frequently brought them face to face with Jewish merchants who had to say no to them. The businessmen were far better able to hide behind the nameless, faceless anonymity of the corporations they dominated.[2]

Though local Jews were never really targeted by the local klavern of the Ku Klux Klan, reported to be the largest in the South, Jews still knew that they had a precarious position in the social scheme of things. In fact, in 1958 several sticks of dynamite had been found at one of the town's synagogues.

The SCLC's Shuttlesworth was aware that local Jews were dedicated to the status quo:

> I think the majority of their congregations—I'm talking about the Deep South now—were real Southern. . . . Not that the majority of their congregations would join a mob; but so far as being for the status quo, so far as voting against the interests of something that would move the Negro forward—the majority was negative.[3]

Essentially, the Jewish position, as articulated by Harold Katz, an official with the Birmingham Jewish Community Center and Jewish Community Council, was that "the racial problem does not call for a resolution on the part of the Jewish community but one by the general community."[4] Katz also claimed "that the Jewish community cannot take the lead unless the general community does so and that all work in this area must be done behind the scenes."[5] But behind-the-scenes activity was indeed taking place.

Birmingham's form of government revolved around "Bull" Connor. Conner ran Birmingham with an iron hand. He was backed by a collection of bullies, who included members of his police department as well as deputized civilians. A black or a white agitating for civil rights never stood a chance.

For the businessmen of Birmingham, the state of terror that Conner had created caused them to try to figure out how to get rid of their dangerous, raging "Bull" without actually confronting him or facing his henchmen. But with Connor recently reelected by a healthy majority of the vote, they feared not only for their physical safety but also for their economic well-being. To circumvent antici-pated problems, they started circulating a petition to change the city government from that of a commissioner to that of a mayor and coun-cil. An election was held—and the majority voted to eliminate the office of public safety.

Connor would not take this usurpation lightly: He ran for the office of mayor. Though he lost, he refused to permit the newly elect-ed mayor to oust him from his office. A legal battle ensued as the courts tried to decide whether to permit Connor to fulfill the balance of his previously elected term of office or to honor the new election, which had abolished that office. In the meantime, the town was divided between the anti- and pro-Connor factions, and Connor pro-ceeded to continue to wreak his racist havoc.

> As the political maneuvering transpired, . . . Shuttlesworth and the Alabama Christian Movement for Human Rights (ACMHR) organized student sit-ins at downtown department stores and met with white business leaders to try to break the barriers around public facilities. These leaders included [Chamber of Commerce President Sidney] Smyer and representatives from the major stores: Sears, Loveman's, Newberry's, Greene's, Woolworth's, and Pizitz. Loveman's and Pizitz, two of the largest, were founded by local Jewish merchants. Although a segregationist, Louis Pizitz had been a longtime supporter of south-ern black institutions. He and the representative from Loveman's played crucial roles at the meeting. Initially, after an awkward silence, Loveman's spokesman offered to "desegregate" his store's water fountains. Shuttlesworth countered that [blacks] were "past water now. We have to have toilets." Another painful silence ensued, and

then black negotiator and businessman A. G. Gaston turned to Loveman's representative and said, "You know, your daddy and I got started in business about the same time. And you know you got your start among the Negroes like I did. We got our money together. And most of our customers are Negroes. And it looks like you could do something." After yet another silence, Shuttlesworth turned to Louis Pizitz: "Mr. Pizitz, the last time, they arrested two students in your store. This time it's gonna be different. Martin Luther King and I are gonna sit on your stool, and we aren't gonna walk out. They're gonna have to drag us out. And the press will be there. And you'll be out of business all over Alabama." While Shuttlesworth and Pizitz "glared" at each other, Loveman's representative responded: "Wait a minute I can just call the maintenance man and just paint over the ['whites only'] sign in the restroom." The impasse had been broken under pressure.[6]

As early as January 1963, King had been gathering the personnel and making the rounds to raise the money necessary for an assault on Birmingham. In New York, at a private party in the apartment of entertainer and actor Harry Belafonte, he was promised the funds for the campaign. At the same time, King was pressuring President Kennedy to send a civil rights bill to Congress. A half-hearted attempt at best, the bill quickly died in Congress. "There wasn't any interest in it," the attorney general, Bobby Kennedy, explained. "There was no public demand for it. There was no demand by the newspapers or radio or television. There was no interest by people coming to watch the hearings. . . . Nobody came. Nobody paid any attention."[7]

And so attention had to be created. Birmingham took center stage. For King, still smarting from his unsuccessful campaign in Albany, Birmingham would be a ripe battlefield for the movement. Though he initially acceded to the demands of local leaders that no action be taken until after the upcoming elections, whatever agreements were made between the white and black community were too little and too late. The three-hundred-year-old credo among whites of "gradual change" would no longer work. On April 3, the campaign began in earnest:

> King issued a "Birmingham Manifesto" . . . [that demanded] that all lunch counters, restrooms, and drinking fountains in downtown department and variety stores be desegregated, that Negroes be hired in local business and industry, and that a biracial committee be established to work out a schedule for desegregation in other areas of city life. Directed at the economic power structure rather than . . . city government, the manifesto warned that demonstrations and boycotts would continue until these demands were met.[8]

Birmingham Rabbi Milton Grafman appealed to King and other civil rights organizers that local Jews were "caught between the Negroes and the Whites—they couldn't win for losing."[9] Grafman's appeal had no effect. For four days, starting on April 6, sit-ins, demonstrations, picketing and boycotts were standard operating procedure. So was the revolving door of getting arrested, paying bail, then getting arrested again. But on April 11, the city got a judge to issue an injunction ordering King and his associates to desist.

Jack Greenberg, head of the NAACP's Legal Defense Fund, later recalled:

> Birmingham had an ordinance requiring a permit, issued by the city commission, to hold a parade. Although it was clearly unconstitutional, setting forth as it did no standards for granting or denial, I counseled SCLC staff to play it safe and apply. I went to the local Western Union office . . . on April 5 and wrote out an application for a permit, which I telegraphed to the notorious Bull Connor. . . . He replied that the entire city commission had to act on a parade permit request. . . . As usual, special procedures had been devised for us; the city clerk, not the commission, routinely issued permits to applicants who were not black protesters.

As Good Friday and Easter Sunday approached, Martin announced that he would march on those symbolically important days. Without notice, the city promptly got a local court to issue a temporary restraining order, which the sheriff served on Martin and his aides at the Gaston Motel at 1:15 A.M. on April 11. The injunction prohibited marching without a permit and incorporated verbatim the local ordinance we believed was unconstitutional—six years later the Supreme Court held we were right in that belief. Later that day, Martin issued a press release announcing that "in good conscience" he could not obey the injunction, "not out of any disrespect for the law but out of the highest respect for the law."[10]

On Good Friday, King and fifty of his associates were arrested for parading without a permit. From New York, Stanley Levison immediately sent a telegram to "Bull" Connor using the pseudonym "Beatrice Murkin:"

Whether you chose to recognize it or not, you have in custody one of the world's formost [sic] citizens, Dr. Martin L. King. Since you were responsible for his arrest, the burden of his safety is in your hands. Our nation would never live down its shame if by some cowardly manouver [sic] he was harmed in your jail.[11]

On April 13, the *Birmingham News* printed an open letter directed to the Birmingham community. But it was obvious to whom it was addressed:

We the undersigned clergymen are among those who, in January, issued "An Appeal for Law and Order and Common Sense," in dealing with racial problems in Alabama. We expressed understanding that honest convictions in racial matters could properly be pursued in the courts, but urged that decisions of those courts should in the meantime be peacefully obeyed.

Since that time there has been some evidence of increased forbearance and a willingness to face facts. Responsible citizens have undertaken to work on various problems which cause racial friction and unrest. In Birmingham, recent public events have given indication that we all have opportunity for a new constructive and realistic approach to racial problems.

However, we are now confronted by . . . demonstrations by some of our Negro citizens, directed and led in part by outsiders. We recognize the natural impatience of people who feel that their hopes are slow in being realized. But . . . these demonstrations are unwise and untimely.

We agree rather with certain local Negro leadership which has called for honest and open negotiation of racial issues in our area. And we believe this kind of facing of issues can best be accomplished by citizens of our own metropolitan area, white and Negro, meeting with their knowledge and experience of the local situation. All of us need to face that responsibility and find proper channels for its accomplishment.

Just as we formerly pointed out that "hatred and violence have no sanction in our religious and political traditions," we also point out that such actions that incite to hatred and violence, however technically peaceful those actions may be, have not contributed to the resolution of our local problems. We do not believe that these days of new hope are days when extreme measures are justified in Birmingham.

We commend the community as a whole, and the local news media and law enforcement officials in particular, on the calm manner in which these demonstrations have been handled. We urge the public to continue to show restraint should the demonstrations continue, and the law enforcement officials to remain calm and continue to protect our city from violence.

We further strongly urge our own Negro community to withdraw support from these demonstrations, and to unite locally in working peacefully for a better Birmingham. When rights are consistently denied, a cause should be pressed in the courts and in negotiations among local leaders, and not in the streets. We appeal to both our white and Negro citizenry to observe the principles of law and order and common sense.[12]

Among the eight clergy who signed the letter was Rabbi Milton L. Grafman of Temple Emanu-El.

King's response to these clergymen became the legendary "Letter from Birmingham City Jail." Though only one Jew had signed the letter in the *Birmingham News,* King pointedly addressed Jewish themes in his response:

> We can never forget that everything Hitler did in Germany was "legal" and everything the Hungarian freedom fighters did in Hungary was "illegal." It was "illegal" to aid and comfort a Jew in Hitler's Germany. But I am sure that if I had lived in Germany during that time I would have aided and comforted my Jewish brothers even though it was illegal. If I lived in a Communist country today where certain principles dear to the Christian faith are suppressed, I believe I would openly advocate disobeying these anti-religious laws. I must make two honest confessions to you, my Christian and Jewish brothers. First, I must confess that over the last few years I have been gravely disappointed with the white moderate. I have almost reached the regrettable conclusion that the Negro's great stumbling block in the stride toward freedom is not the White Citizen's Council or the Ku Klux Klanner, but the white moderate who is more devoted to "order" than to justice; who prefers a negative peace which is the absence of tension to a positive peace which is the presence of justice; who constantly says, "I agree with you in the goal you seek, but I can't agree with your methods of direct action"; who paternalistically feels that he can set the timetable for another man's freedom; who lives by the myth of time and who constantly advises the Negro to wait until a "more convenient season." Shallow understanding from people of good will is more frustrating than absolute misunderstanding from people of ill will. Lukewarm acceptance is much more bewildering than outright rejection.[13]

Chastising the eight clergy who had signed the letter in the paper, King admitted that he had anticipated that the white ministers, priests and rabbis of the South would be among our strongest allies. Instead, some have been outright opponents, refusing to understand the freedom movement and misrepresenting its leaders; all too many others have been more cautious than courageous and have remained silent behind the anesthetizing security of stained-glass windows.

In spite of my shattered dreams, I came to Birmingham with the hope that the white religious leadership of this community would see the justice of our cause and, with deep moral concern, would serve as the channel through which our just grievances could reach the power structure. I had hoped that each of you would understand. But again I have been disappointed.[14]

Released from prison on April 20, King faced a depleted campaign: few volunteers, no money, and another court appointment in May. As for Rabbi Grafman, he would never regret participating in the attack on King. At a convention of the Reform Movement's Central Conference of America Rabbis proclaiming equal opportunity for blacks, Grafman told his fellow rabbis to reconsider their holier-than-thou attitudes:

My colleagues who have shouted the loudest have not been willing to take southern pulpits—period. . . . They like their fifteen and twenty thousand dollar pulpits. . . . If you are truly sincere about your prophetic Judaism, then you would not hesitate to take a pulpit in Gadsden, Alabama, for $9,000 a year. This is what a prophet does. But he has no right to tell somebody else to commit economic suicide unless he's willing to make a sacrifice himself.[15]

In the middle of all this, the real battle of Birmingham began. Members of King's staff had been canvassing college campuses for new recruits. Soon high school students joined in, and they brought their little brothers and sisters. Their appearance inspired a plan put forward by long-time SCLC stalwart James Bevel. As one participant, lawyer William Kunstler, later explained:

> When he was released [from prison], Martin called a meeting in his room at Gaston's Motel—the famous Room 30 where all the strategy sessions were held—to deal with a peril to the Birmingham operation. Bull Connor had carried out his threat to arrest all demonstrators, and as a result, there simply were not enough adults remaining in the community to march. Spirits were low, perhaps the lowest they had been since the Birmingham crusade had begun only weeks earlier.
>
> There was quite a bit of friction in the room when it looked as if the movement were running out of bodies to fill the jails; Fred Shuttlesworth was angry, and Martin was despondent, fearful that the operation was failing. I was uncomfortable; I could think of no way to help. Suddenly, . . . James Bevel, a small man with a bald pate and fiery eyes, spoke up.
>
> "Why don't we ask the schoolchildren to start marching? Let's keep them out of school and have them fill the ranks," Bevel suggested. Initially, most of the people in the room were not in favor of this radical idea. It would be too dangerous; children should not be exposed to arrests and beatings, they said. But Bevel persisted. "We're doing what we're doing for the next generation, so why shouldn't the kids join the struggle?"
>
> "Children marching might draw more attention to our protest," I added. Gradually, everyone agreed to Bevel's plan. A message was sent to ministers and other community leaders that parents should keep their children home from school so that the youngsters could pick up the banner and march as their elders had done.[16]

On May 2, more than a thousand children marched. Over nine hundred were arrested. The next day, twenty-five hundred children marched. On this day, the name of "Bull" Connor would be enshrined in the halls of infamy. As police dogs strained against their leashes and firemen unrolled hose lines, newspaper reporters and TV cameras recorded what happened next. At Connor's command, the dogs were let loose and the high-pressure fire hoses were opened. The children were flung everywhere as dogs bit and maimed them. A stunned world reacted in outrage.

The next day, the carnage continued: children marching and singing, dogs attacking, water hoses pummeling them. On May 5, three thousand children marched. But the police and firefighters could not continue. They stood there—frozen. As King later said, "It was one of the most fantastic events of the Birmingham story. I saw there, I felt there, for the first time, the pride and the power of nonviolence."[17]

With three thousand people in jail and another four thousand waiting their turn, Director of Public Safety Al Lingo petitioned Governor George Wallace for the use of state troopers. As the situation threatened to explode even further, secret negotiations were taking place to end the stand-off. Even Burke Marshall of President Kennedy's staff had come to town to negotiate with the parties involved. In the meantime, King issued an appeal for the entire nation to bear witness to the horrors taking place in Birmingham.

As King searched for witnesses in his Birmingham battle, twenty rabbis left the sixty-third annual convention of the Conservative movement's Rabbinical Assembly to fly to Birmingham and join King. At the convention, Rabbi Bernard Mandelbaum had challenged his colleagues to answer whether they only concern themselves with Nazi cruelty "when acts of injustice to fellow human beings were taking place in our country." When they called the Southern Christian Leadership Conference in Atlanta, they were told that their presence in the South was urgent and important. A. D. King, Martin's brother, urged them "this is the time to come."[18]

For many Jews in Birmingham, the presence of these rabbis was deeply disturbing. Fearing that Jewish participation in any demonstration would only spur criticism of the local Jewish population, and maybe even provoke violence against it, they asked the would-be demonstrators to leave. "Two of the rabbis [who had just arrived in Birmingham] met with the group until dawn. What they heard was the story of a Jewish community in panic. For months, King had led an economic boycott on the downtown which had all but destroyed the Jewish store owners. . . . In addition, several sticks of dynamite with a faulty fuse had been discovered on the steps of . . . [a] synagogue, and . . . [local Jewish leaders were] asking the rabbis to return home before they involved the Jewish community any deeper in turmoil."[19]

After settling in their motel, the rabbis met with King. As one rabbi who was there remembered:

> When he came in, we saw a very tired young man. At arm's-length he looked younger, leaner, shorter, much more vulnerable than at some distance or in his public image. There was great weariness and something close to physical pain on his lips. But his smile was warm and wholly sincere all the same. As though he had no other worry in the world, he contemplated and answered our questions, endured the speech-makings that a few of us . . . found it impossible to resist. . . . We must have spent about one hour with Dr. King . . . He spoke of his disappointment in so-called white liberals and their temporizing, also in the failure of most of the clergy to take an unequivocal stand on the side of racial equality and integration. . . . [H]e quoted Martin Buber and the Hebrew Bible; and when, at our request, he led us in a parting prayer, there was a sacred stillness in the air.[20]

That night the rabbis participated in services at local black churches. Remarked one, "When we entered their churches, we were greeted as 'our rabbis,' as if we were a precious possession. We marched down the aisles amid standing and cheering congregations."[21]

Rabbi Richard Rubenstein later remarked:

> The Negro community saw the rabbis in a way in which they had sel-
> dom seen Jews. By our very presence we were handing down a kind
> of "apostolic" succession to them. We were saying that the flesh and
> blood children of Israel were behind them in their struggle, that we
> had gone from slavery to freedom, and we knew they would. The
> convention behind the symbolism of solidarity was heightened by our
> willingness to incur risks of physical harm to bear witness to our con-
> victions.[22]

As plans were broadcast for a march that Friday, a panicked group of local Jewish leaders met again with some of the rabbis in the offices of attorney Karl Freedman. The discussion soon bordered on the hysterical:

> Freedman started the meeting off with a determined plea to the rab-
> bis that ended with, "You'll kill my wife and daughters"; at one point,
> a participant remembered that one of the rabbis said, "The Jews have
> too long been passive; we know the risks; we may be shot at, but it is
> time." [One of the Birmingham participants] Dora Roth remembers
> telling them, "You will go back on the plane heroes and leave us to
> gather the wrath. I hope your convictions are strong enough to carry
> the blood of my children on your hands."
>
> "The contact was an aching one," wrote Rabbi Andre Ungar of
> Westwood, New Jersey. . . . "What seemed to stun them most ago-
> nizingly was the realization that we were at the call of the Negro
> leadership rather than vice versa. It appeared to outrage the natural
> order of things."[23]

Their presence had helped focus more national attention on Birmingham. As negotiations between blacks and local business leaders proceeded, the rabbis returned home. Though they left behind a legacy of confusion and hostility in the community they had hoped to positively affect, Birmingham would remain a high point of their lives. Rabbi Jack Bloom said:

> Reverend Ralph Abernathy, at a rally held in a church, . . . told how
> Moses avoided looking at the [burning] bush. God finally forced
> Moses to look at the bush, and Moses looked at it until the fire of that
> bush burned within him. With that fire within, Moses took the first
> steps towards redeeming his people. I think that many of us felt that
> way about our "Birmingham" experience. Something about those
> days transformed our brothers' burning desire for freedom and
> equality into a flame burning within us.[24]

On May 10, an agreement was announced: Within ninety days, every aspect of tenets of King's Birmingham Manifesto would be implemented. As King flew home to celebrate Mother's Day and to preach at his own church, things literally blew up. That night, the Gaston Motel and the home of A.D. King were dynamited. Martin Luther King rushed back to Birmingham, and President Kennedy positioned three thousand federal troops outside the city and announced that he was calling up the Alabama National Guard.

Four months later, on September 15, a bomb exploded at the Sixteenth Street Baptist Church during Sunday services. Four young girls were killed. King returned to Birmingham to attend the funeral. Milton Grafman was one of the clergy in attendance. To John T. Porter, the minister of the Sixth Avenue Baptist Church where the funeral was held, the service saw "the largest outpouring of clergy across Christian-Jewish lines dressed in clergy garb ever before or since. . . . I felt great joy in seeing the togetherness of leaders of the religious community, but great sadness that it took this event to bring us together."[25]

Later, Grafman helped create a fund to pay for the victims' funerals, for the hospital bills of those injured in the explosion, and for the reconstruction of the Sixteenth Street church. He would remain, as he was before King had come to Birmingham, a staunch advocate of equal rights and interreligious cooperation. But even after he died in 1995, the stigma of King's campaign remained to diminish Grafman's own legacy.[26]

10

All Eyes on Washington

By the summer of 1963, blacks, who had been on the margins of American politics and society for so long, were beginning to emerge from years of repression. But segregation was still strong and flourishing in the South, and social and economic discrimination certainly persisted in the North. Meanwhile, the Kennedy White House had become a bit of a disappointment to the civil rights movement: Contrary to expectations, it was not exactly breaking down the doors of Southern classrooms to let black children in or trying to foster economic opportunity for blacks across the nation.

For this reason, under the aegis of A. Philip Randolph and Bayard Rustin, plans were made for a massive march on Washington. To be held on August 28, it would demand that Kennedy and Congress support legislation granting blacks full rights. A. Philip Randolph, head of the Brotherhood of Sleeping Car Porters, had contemplated such a march back in the 1940s, but it had never materialized. Now, with Abraham Lincoln's Emancipation Proclamation reaching its centennial, Randolph wanted to bring a mass march to Washington to bring attention to "unfulfilled social and economic promises of a hundred years."[1]

A Jewish response to the planned march was mandatory. As Rabbi Richard Hirsch wrote a few years later in the journal of the Central Conference of American Rabbis, the umbrella organization of Reform rabbis,

> In Jewish tradition, salvation for the individual is inseparable from salvation for all mankind, personal ethics are inseparable from social ethics, and in our day social ethics are inseparable from social action.
>
> But knowing when and how to engage in social action is not easy. Social issues are extremely complex. It is only . . . in retrospect that the moral dimension becomes obvious to everyone. . . . When we look back on the August 1963 March on Washington, there . . . [is] overwhelming support for the contention that the participation of so many of our rabbis and laymen was both moral and in consonance with Jewish tradition. A month before the march we were not so sure. There was great trepidation as to the political ramifications, as to whether or not it would be good for the cause. There was fear of violence, and potentially a situation in which we would have engaged in illegal acts. . . .
>
> To decide not to act is also a decision. It was Cato who said, "Never is one so active as when one does nothing." And it was our rabbis who said "He who learns without doing something about it, it would have been better if he had not been born." The fact is that on most issues, we do not take positions. In instances when we do engage in social action, we in effect declare that the risk of no action is greater than the risk of mistaken action. If theology has its leap of faith, social justice must have its leap of action.[2]

And so, a leap of action took place, and Jews soon took up the call for the march. The American Jewish Committee stated in the weeks leading up to the march that the Emancipation Proclamation's pledge of first-class citizenship and freedom for the American Negro remains tragically unfulfilled. This enormous gap between promise and actuality underscores the justifiable impatience with which Negroes are insistently demanding their full democratic rights now. As members of a group . . . which has from time immemorial known oppression and felt the indignities of discrimination, Jews understand the frustrations experienced by our Negro fellow citizens. We share with them the determination to eliminate swiftly the injustices from which they suffer.

The . . . March on Washington . . . will demonstrate the deep commitment of a vast majority of the American people to the attainment of full equality for all. . . . [We] wholeheartedly endorse the March, as have the leading Protestant and Catholic agencies. We believe the March to be in the greatest tradition of peaceable assembly for a redress of grievances and therefore vigorously support local affiliates throughout the nation who desire to participate in this historic event.

The Jews have always been part of the eternal quest for human dignity and social justice for all mankind. Our devotion to this cause is rooted deeply in our religious and spiritual traditions and our social experience. A most appropriate means of expressing our ideals today, as Americans and Jews, consists in joining together with all men of good will in this peaceful and lawful assembly for the realization of a more humane and democratic society.[3]

The Committee sent notices to its members, especially in the South, advising that "peaceful demonstrations are a proper and, indeed, characteristically American means of petitioning government for the redress of grievances and for fulfilling rights guaranteed to all Americans. We therefore call on AJC members to participate in this peaceful demonstration."[4]

Then the day finally arrived. Despite the critics, despite the hardships, and despite the fear of potential violence, the marchers came from all over the nation: over 250,000 people, the largest group in the history of the civil rights movement and one of the largest demonstrations ever held in Washington. From its meeting point at the base of the Washington monument, the crowd marched to the Lincoln Memorial. Actor Charlton Heston, one of a contingent of Hollywood stars who had made the trip, said, "We will march because we recognize the events of the summer of 1963 as among the most significant we have lived through; and we wish to be part of these events and these times, when promises made a century ago will finally be kept."[5]

On the platform were the leaders of the major Jewish-American organizations, including Shad Polier of the American Jewish Congress, Rabbi Leon Foyer of the Central Conference of American Rabbis, George Maislan of the United Synagogue of America, and Rabbi Uri Miller of the Synagogue Council of America. Below them, thousands of other Jews mingled with other whites and blacks. Conservative Jews marched under the banner of the United Synagogue of America; Reform Jews carried signs with the quote from Leviticus (in both Hebrew and English) that was inscribed in 1751 on the Liberty Bell: "Proclaim liberty throughout the land, and unto all the inhabitants thereof" (Lev. 25:1); other Jews carried signs that read, "We march together, Catholics, Jews and Protestants."[6]

The program began with representatives from several religious groups offering opening prayers. Rabbi Uri Miller, president of the Synagogue Council of America, prayed that those assembled would not voice empty words "nor even sincere ideals projected into some Messianic future, but actualities expressed in our society in concrete and tangible form now." He hoped that the demonstration would "sensitize all Americans and especially those in positions of power and authority to this concept of equality" and asked for the nation to understand that "when we deprive our fellowman of bread and dignity, we negate the *Tselem Elokim*—the image of God in man—and delay the fulfillment of His Kingdom."[7]

Then came an assortment of other speakers, one after another. John Lewis of SNCC, who had been beaten and almost left for dead in several civil rights demonstrations in the South, reminded the marchers that they were "involved in a serious social revolution. . . . What political leader can stand up and say, 'My party is the party of principles?' For the party of Kennedy is also the party of [Mississippi senator James] Eastland. The party of [New York's liberal senator, Jacob] Javits is also the party of [Arizona's conservative senator, Barry] Goldwater. Where is *our* party? Where is the political party that will make it unnecessary to march on Washington? Where is the political party that will make it unnecessary to march on the streets of Birmingham?" A. Philip Randolph introduced women who had led the fight they were all celebrating: Rosa Parks, Daisy Bates, Diane Nash Bevel, Gloria Richardson. Marian Anderson sang "He's Got the Whole World in His Hands," and Mahalia Jackson followed her with "I Been 'Buked and I Been Scorned." Finally, Rabbi Joachim Prinz, head of the American Jewish Congress, who spoke after Rev. Jesse Jackson, declared, "When I was the rabbi of the Jewish community in Berlin under the Hitler regime, I learned many things. The most important thing that I learned . . . is that bigotry and hatred are not the most urgent problem. The most urgent, the most disgraceful, the most shameful and the most tragic problem is silence."[8]

The speeches went on interminably, and at last it was King's turn to bring the program to a close. As the assembly listened, and as millions watched on their television sets, King delivered one of the grandest, most eloquent, most personal speeches of his life:

I have a dream that one day every valley shall be exalted, every hill and mountain shall be made low, the rough places shall be made plain, and the crooked places shall be made straight and the glory of the Lord will be revealed and all flesh shall see it together. . . . With this faith we will be able to hew out of the mountain of despair a stone of hope. With this faith we will be able to transform the jangling discords of our nation into a beautiful symphony of brotherhood.

With this faith we will be able to work together, to pray together, to struggle together, to go to jail together, to stand up for freedom together, knowing that we will be free one day. This will be the day when all of God's children will be able to sing with new meaning— "my country 'tis of thee; sweet land of liberty; of thee I sing; land where my fathers died, land of the pilgrim's pride; from every mountain side, let freedom ring"—and if America is to be a great nation, this must become true....And when we allow freedom to ring, when we let it ring from every village and hamlet, from every state and city, we will be able to speed up that day when all of God's children— black men and white men, Jews and Gentiles, Catholics and Protestants—will be able to join hands and to sing in the words of the old Negro spiritual, "Free at last, free at last: thank God Almighty, we are free at last."[9]

The march ensured that King was a national figure as he had never been before, that his influence and stature were, indeed, almost the equal of the monarch that his name implied. It also convincingly showed the Kennedy administration that it must act against racism and segregation despite the deeply entrenched Southern (and in many cases Northern) opposition to change. Kennedy would never have a chance to present a clear and definitive program to Congress that would accomplish this. On November 22, 1963—barely three months after the march—the young president was assassinated.

11

Freedom Summer, 1964

Among the many Jews who involved themselves in the civil rights movement, Allard Lowenstein was one of the most enigmatic. Educated at the University of North Carolina and Yale Law School, by 1959 he was a foreign policy aide to Minnesota Senator Hubert Humphrey. Having ventured into South Africa to examine the suppression of its blacks for a United Nations commission, by 1962 Lowenstein was a 32-year-old assistant dean and political science lecturer at Stanford University, encouraging students to become engaged with such causes as protesting apartheid. The activist legacy he left behind in Stanford seemed to culminate in one week in May 1963: During those seven days, Rabbi Abraham Joshua Heschel, an intimate of King's, gave several lectures on humanity's search for meaning; novelist James Baldwin spoke on race; and there was a mass rally in support of the black children who had been attacked by dogs and fire hoses on the streets of Birmingham.[1]

Throughout his life, Lowenstein would show up in places to "help," start trouble, and then depart before he could be held accountable. His activities at Stanford were no exception, and had quickly made him persona non grata. Typical of the way Lowenstein did things was his attempt to get service at a restaurant in a very prestigious segregated hotel in North Carolina, the Sir Walter. Seated with him was a black acquaintance: Liberia's ambassador to the United Nations. Lowenstein's failure to identify the black man as an ambassador infuriated the State Department, whose officials were infuriated by their perception that Lowenstein had deliberately tried to provoke an international incident because the diplomat had legal immunity from North Carolina's segregation laws.[2]

In early 1962, several civil rights organizations—SCLC, SNCC, CORE, NAACP—had organized under the banner of the newly formed Council of Federated Organizations (COFO) so they could present as strung and coordinated a front as possible in Mississippi, considered by these organizations to be the most recalcitrant, racist state in the country. Headed by veteran civil rights worker Bob Moses, COFO was staffed primarily by SNCC volunteers.

Lowenstein heard about COFO's plans and decided that Mississippi would be his next port of call. Then teaching at the University of North Carolina, he journeyed to COFO headquarters in Jackson, Mississippi, in July 1963 and offered his help to Moses. It wasn't long before the two had conceived a plan to hold a mock election to test the effectiveness of COFO's voter registration program. Without the constraints imposed by the Mississippi racist electoral system, the "freedom vote" attracted a sizeable black turnout. Encouraged by the success, a more ambitious scheme was put into action to demonstrate the corrupt voting practices in Mississippi, which were putting only white candidates into office.

Moses bought into a Lowenstein plan to recruit Northern college students to help in COFO's election initiatives. Then he had second thoughts about the project, because

> bringing a reforming army of white college students to Mississippi might well mean sending some of them to their deaths. And because such ... violence against whites would help bring Mississippi to the attention of the rest of the country—a movement objective—Moses was confronted with a question of moral responsibility. If he was going to be honest, he had to acknowledge that getting white people killed in the movement's name was part of the reason for inviting them. Indeed, the idea was not just to bring any whites to Mississippi, but "the best" young people in America, the sons and daughters of politicians and of prominent families, students at the nation's most prestigious schools—Harvard, Yale, Stanford, Columbia, and Princeton, among others. Camus's ideal, "be neither victim nor executioner," no doubt weighed increasingly on Moses' mind. Was there simply no moral ground available between the two roles?[3]

Lowenstein had no such trepidations, and he began recruiting students even before getting formal COFO approval. Among those who traveled south that summer were a 21-year-old New Yorker who was studying at Queens College, Andrew Goodman; 24-year-old Michael Schwerner and his wife, Rita, civil rights workers for CORE; and James Chaney, a 21-year-old black from Meridian, Mississippi, who had left high school five years before and had only recently become involved with the civil rights movement.

The three young men were trained for their work in Mississippi at a series of workshops in Oxford, Ohio, then drove south together. Just a few months before, after the 1964 Civil Rights Act was passed, Ross Barnett, the state's ex-governor, had warned, "This action is repulsive to the American people. Turmoil, strife, and blood lie ahead."

Barnett was both prescient, and an instigator. Goodman, Schwerner, and Chaney—two Jews and a Christian—arrived in Mississippi on June 20. Around 11 A.M. the next day, they got into their blue Ford station wagon and headed to nearby Longdale to investigate a recent church burning and the beating of church members. The Ku Klux Klan, which was active in the area, had been burning down churches and otherwise intimidating anyone involved with voter registration campaigns. The civil rights workers said they would be back by 4 P.M. that afternoon. They were never seen again—alive. They vanished on a Sunday. Police in the town of Philadelphia said they had stopped Chaney for speeding, detained Schwerner and Goodman for "investigation" for six hours, and released all three of them after they had spent six hours in jail. In another two days, President Lyndon Johnson sent Allen Dulles, the former head of the FBI, to Mississippi to coordinate the investigation for the missing men. Two hundred agents and four hundred sailors from a Mississippi naval air station were assigned to the case.

About six weeks after the men had vanished, three bodies were found in an earthen dam not too far from Philadelphia. Fingerprints and dental plates identified them as Schwerner, Chaney, and Goodman.

The murders, Jonathan Kaufman wrote in *Broken Alliance*, his account of black-Jewish relations, were

a powerful symbol, but—like many symbols—it masked a great deal of complexity. A confluence of events had brought blacks and Jews together. History, recent experiences in America, and the trauma of the Holocaust in Europe had shaped the Jewish vision as ally to the underdog. The message offered by King—that people be judged not on their skin color or religion, but on the content of their character and their merits—appealed to them. The rhetoric of World War II and the burgeoning Cold War persuaded black leaders that now was again the time to work with white allies. . . .

[T]he impulse behind the cooperation of Jews and blacks was genuine, and so were the friendships and the relationships that grew out of the cooperation. After their son's body was found with the bodies of Mickey Schwerner and Jim Chaney, Carolyn and Robert Goodman decided to help Chaney's mother and her youngest son move north from Mississippi. They helped find Fannie Chaney an apartment on Columbus Avenue, a few blocks from where the Goodmans lived, and helped her find a job. They raised scholarship money so her son Ben, who had met Andy over dinner the night before he disappeared, could go to Andy's old private school on New York's Upper West Side. "We wanted to help that family as much as we could," Carolyn Goodman told me more than twenty years later. "We wanted to help make a difference in their lives."[4]

In the meantime, the SNCC workers in Mississippi were getting increasingly frustrated with Lowenstein's grandstanding. He was constantly calling newspapers or famous people or raising funds for the cause, often presenting himself as one of the strategic masterminds behind the Mississippi Summer Project. His behavior soon cost him his relationship with SNCC, exactly at a moment when SNCC's blacks were tiring of having whites be among the top leaders in their own organizations. Lowenstein also represented to them the forces of reasonable moderation, a stance that SNCC was on the verge of rejecting. As James Forman, then SNCC's executive secretary, said, Lowenstein "represented a whole body of influential forces seeking to prevent SNCC from becoming too radical and bring it under . . . control."[5]

Rabbi Arthur Lelyveld, a volunteer from Cleveland, was bludgeoned by thugs during a COFO-sponsored program in Hattiesburg, and as more and more whites found themselves jailed, beaten, and literally run out of one town after another, and as one church after another was dynamited, the summer project proceeded to sign up black voters. With eighty thousand signatories, the Mississippi

Freedom Democratic Party (MFDP) was established to challenge the white-only Mississippi delegates who were heading to the Democratic Party's national convention in Atlantic City.

Lowenstein was asked by the MFDP to act as a lobbyist for its cause at the convention. Because of his connections and influence in the Democratic Party, it was hoped that an attempt to unseat the so-called Jim Crow delegates (those who discriminated against Negroes) from Mississippi might be successful.

The group had earlier retained Washington insider and long-term Jewish activist Joseph Rauh to be their attorney. Rauh was a prominent figure in liberal Democratic politics, a founding member of Americans for Democratic Action (ADA), and a longtime supporter of the civil rights movement. At the 1948 Democratic National Convention, Rauh had helped Hubert Humphrey get a strong civil rights plank adopted into the party's platform. In 1963 and 1964, he had been a key lobbyist for the Civil Rights Act. In short, Rauh's progressive credentials were impeccable, so when he rose to address the convention's credentials committee on August 22, 1964, people listened. He summoned a series of witnesses to Mississippi's brutality: Rita Schwerner, James Farmer, Roy Wilkins, Aaron Henry, and Rev. Edwin King, the last of whom testified, "I have been imprisoned, I have been beaten, I have been close to death. The Freedom Party is an open party. They" — pointing to the spokesmen for the Mississippi Democratic regulars — "are a closed party of a closed society."[6]

The credentials committee hearings, which were televised, helped the MFDP get more support from around the country. But Lyndon Johnson had the Mississippi Freedom delegates bugged — and learned in advance all of their tactics. Using Hubert Humphrey as his spokesperson, Johnson proposed a compromise that would let two of the MFDP delegates be seated as delegates-at-large. The group rejected the offer — and the MFDP campaign was swiftly lost.

At a meeting of the allies of the Mississippi Summer Project afterward, Mendy Samstein of SNCC accused Bayard Rustin of being a traitor; Joe Rauh was torn by his loyalty to his liberal colleagues from Washington who had orchestrated the MFDP's defeat—and his commitment to his black clients; and Walter Reuther of the United Auto Workers felt betrayed by Martin Luther King for not using his influence to have the compromise accepted. Lowenstein was charged as an influence peddler who had sold out the movement for his own gain, since he had favored the compromise.

In 1967, Lowenstein hosted a meeting at Granson's, his family's restaurant in Manhattan, to discuss the possibility of forming a third party in the upcoming election that would be adamantly against the war. Among those present were James Wechsler, a left-center columnist for the *New York Post*, and Norman Thomas, the Socialist who had run for president several times himself. Representing King was Andrew Young. Lowenstein wanted King to be the party's candidate, an idea that did not catch fire with the group, partly because running a black—especially King—would blur the would-be party's anti-war mission. And anyway, Young said, King would not run under any circumstances.[7]

Lowenstein never gave up on politics or on his own mesmerizing ability to get things done, to change the world, to make it into the image he was always dreaming of. In 1978, after he had spent years running off and on for various posts and persuading other people to run, like Eugene McCarthy in 1968 against Lyndon Johnson, New York's fourth congressional district on Long Island finally sent Lowenstein to Congress. Two years later, an old friend of his, Dennis Sweeney, visited him in his Manhattan office. A former honors student at Stanford, Sweeney had been one of Lowenstein's protégés and had followed him to Mississippi during the summer of 1963. When the two returned to Stanford, Sweeney was Lowenstein's chief recruiter in getting students to join them the next summer for Mississippi Freedom Vote. Students thought that Sweeney almost worshiped Lowenstein; one student who balked at going to Mississippi was menacingly told by Sweeney, "Al's not going to be very happy."

In the last 1960s, Sweeney began to exhibit signs of extreme mental problems, telling friends that he saw movies in his head and heard voices and that electrodes had been implanted in his body to control him.

During the 1970s, Lowenstein had seen Sweeney about three times. He'd heard about the younger man's problems, so when Sweeney called for a meeting, Lowenstein agreed to see him, hoping he could perhaps help him. After the two had talked privately in Lowenstein's office for ten minutes, Sweeney pulled a brand-new, seven-shot Llama .380 automatic pistol out of his pocket. He fired all seven shots at Lowenstein, who died that night after an operation lasting five and a half hours. Sweeney told police that Lowenstein had been controlling his mind for years, and he finally had to put an end to it.

"The irony of Al's death," later said Peter Yarrow of the singing group Peter, Paul and Mary, "was that [he was] someone who let crazies into his life . . . [and] believed in his capacity to go into the den of wolves and emerge unscathed. . . . In a sense, he was killed by his own hand."[8]

12

"Our Marching Steps Will Thunder: We Survive!"

As late as the 1960s, there hadn't been much change in the lives of the Jews in the Soviet Union since the days of the czars. Though outright pogroms had ended, discrimination against Jews was virtually official government policy, and they were second-class citizens in their own country.

Such was their suffering that years earlier, the Berditchever Reb had interrupted a Rosh Hashanah service to cry out in Yiddish:

Good Morning to You, Lord Master of the Universe!
I, Levi Yitzhak, son of Sarah of Berditchev,
I come to You with a Din Torah from Your people Israel.
What do You want of Your people Israel?
What have You demanded of Your people Israel?
For everywhere I look it says, "Say unto the children of Israel,"
And every other verse says, "Speak unto the children of Israel,"

And over and over—"Command the children of Israel."
Father, sweet Father in heaven,
How many nations are there in the world? Persians—
    Babylonians—Edomites.
The Russians, what do they say? That their Czar is the
    only ruler.
The Prussians, what do they say? That their Kaiser is supreme.
And the English, what do they say?
That George the third [sic] is the sovereign.
And I, Levi Yitzhak, son of Sarah of Berditchev, say,
"Yisgadal veyiskadash shmay rabbah . . .
Magnified and sanctified is only Thy name."

And I, Levi Yitzhak, son of Sarah of Berditchev, say,
"From my stand I will not waver,
And from this place I shall not move
Until there be an end to all this.
Yisgadal, veyiskadash, shmay rabbah.
Magnified and sanctified is only Thy name.[1]

This song resonated in the hearts of the persecuted Jews who were scattered throughout Eastern Europe, and in time with Jews in America and Israel, because it gave voice to Jews' misery and grandeur, tragedy and glory. Others cherished this song, too, because in it they found the hope of the human soul for freedom and respect.

One of those who heard it was the great American singer Paul Robeson. As a black man whose idealism had spurred him to cry out against injustice and discrimination and who was ostracized by the people of his own country, Robeson incorporated Rabbi Levi Yitzhak's lament into his performances. In 1949, while in Moscow for the 150th anniversary of the birth of the Russian poet Pushkin, he was especially uncomfortable over his inability to find the Jewish friends whom he had visited on previous visits. One prominent Jewish actor-director, Solomon Mikhoels, had been brutally murdered the previous year; after Robeson repeatedly protested that he wanted to see Itik Feffer, the Jewish writer was brought unaccompanied to Robeson's Moscow hotel room. Through mute gestures, Feffer told Robeson that the room was bugged, and the two just swapped pleasantries while communicating important issues through notes and hand symbols. Robeson learned that Mikhoels had been killed by the secret police, that a spate of Jewish cultural figures had been arrested, that Feffer would probably also be killed. He got this message across to Robeson by drawing a finger across his throat. Three years later, he was shot.[2]

Robeson was scheduled to sing in one of Moscow's largest concert halls. The event in mid-June was filled with influential military and government officials—and many Jews. When Robeson included the Kaddish of Rabbi Levi Yitzhak on the list of songs he planned to sing to the committee sponsoring the concert, he received a note from them: "No one in the audience understands Yiddish. It would therefore be out of place to sing any Jewish songs this evening."

Robeson was furious. Of course people understood Yiddish: the most recent Russian census listed Yiddish as the mother tongue of 35 percent of the Jews, who, Robeson knew, would be well represented in the audience. And how many people in the audience would understand the African songs that he would sing in the languages of Ghana and the Congo?

Robeson began the concert in his usual manner, explaining each song when he came to it. The songs from Congo and Ghana, for instance, he said, reflected the anti-colonial and anti-imperialistic mood in those countries. Then, he boldly announced: "And now I shall sing for you a song which has not yet been sung on the concert stage here. It was written about 150 years ago by a Russian citizen who protested against the Czarist regime and who expressed the pain and sorrow of his people in a spiritual plea. The name of the Russian citizen is Levi Yitzhak, and he lived in Berditchev."

Then he began to sing Rabbi Levi Yitzhak's Kaddish. Weeping could be heard from all parts of the audience, especially when he came to these words:

I, Levi Yitzhak, son of Sarah of Berditchev, say:
From this place I shall not move;
From this spot I shall not budge,
Until there be an end to all this.

Robeson sang another song in Yiddish—the resistance song from the Warsaw Ghetto:

Never say that you have reached the very end,
When leaden skies a bitter future may portend,
For sure the hour for which we yearn will yet arrive,
And our marching steps will thunder: we survive!

Tears flowed down dozens of faces. The applause, at first sporadic, reached a crescendo as people came up to the stage to embrace Robeson.[3]

(Unfortunately, Robeson's protest against Soviet anti-Semitism was more symbolic than substantive. When asked about anti-Semitism in the USSR after returning to the United States, he told a journalist, "I met Jewish people all over the place . . . I heard no word about it." He insisted that the Soviets "had done everything" for their national minorities. As late as 1958, after more Jewish cultural figures had been executed, he was, according to his son, "under no illusions about what had happened and what was happening then, as a matter of fact." Apparently, Robeson's insistence that the Soviet Union promised a grand new era for humanity blinded him to the consequences and the dangers of its anti-Semitism.)[4]

Residing with the postwar Soviet Union was an immense multiethnic and multiracial conglomeration of peoples: Mongols, Tartars, and Slavs, literally hundreds of peoples from all of the subjugated countries that constituted the USSR. Yet, despite being Soviet citizens, one group was always singled out for special treatment by the Soviet proletariat. Much like the blacks of America, Russia's Jews, the third largest Jewish population in the world, were always treated as second-class citizens: They had to practice their religion almost covertly, they could barely meet together as Jews, Bibles were not available for them; *matzot* could not be baked; there were no kosher meat shops in the entire USSR, and no Hebrew teachers or schools. One rabbinical seminary existed, with a student body consisting of one single student. By the late 1950s and 1960s, individual Jews

> were being accused of black-marketing and other crimes, forced to "confess" through torture, convicted by their confessions and executed; most of the synagogues had been closed; teaching of Jewish subjects was not permitted; participation in Jewish rites was forbidden; and Jews were not allowed to emigrate from the Soviet Union.[5]

In addition, the government was fostering anti-Semitism through such publications as Trofim Kichko's notorious *Judaism Without Embellishment*, which was published by the Ukrainian Soviet Socialist Republic. In 1964, the newspaper of the Soviet Communist Party, *Izvestiya*, praised the book for "us[ing] new material in analyzing the reactionary nature of Judaism as a form of religious ideology." This so-called "scientific" work depicted Judaism as promoting hypocrisy, bribery, greed, and usury. "What is the secular God of the Jews?" Kichko asked. "Money. Money, that is the jealous God of Israel." Moreover, the Jewish bourgeoisie was motivated by "the chauvinistic idea of the God-chosenness of the Jewish people, the propaganda of messianism and the idea of ruling over the peoples of the world. . . . The ideologists of Judaism, through the 'Holy Scriptures,' teach the observant Jews to hate people of another faith and even destroy them."[6]

In the early 1960s, American Jews began to organize protests against the Soviet government for the way it was treating its Jews. Moshe Decter, one of the earliest pioneers in publicizing the situation of Soviet Jewry, found a sympathetic spirit in Rabbi Abraham Joshua Heschel.

> In August 1962, [there was] a meeting in New York City . . . [where] Heschel drew attention to the fact that one-third of the world's Jewish population was denied the right to live as Jews or to return to their homeland. "Political experts may rebuke us for calling attention to a minor issue when major issues are at stake," Heschel professed, "yet the process of liquidating a great Jewish community is not a minor issue. Should we not be ready to go to jail in order to end the martyrdom of our Russian brethren . . . to arrange sit-ins, protests, days of fasting and prayer, public demonstrations to which even Russian leaders will not remain indifferent? The voice of our brother's agony is crying to us! How can we be silent? How can we remain passive? How can we have peace of mind or live with our conscience?"[7]

Soon, at the 1962 Convention of the United Synagogue of America, the organization of Conservative congregations, Martin Luther King stated regarding Soviet Jewry: "All life is interrelated and we are caught in an inescapable mutuality and a wrong against one is a wrong against all."[8]

As a result, Decter, who was the director of the New York-based Jewish Minorities Research, wrote to King about a project he had been "mulling over": a national conference on Soviet Jewry. King was asked to be a participant. He agreed.

In August 1963, Rabbi Irving Miller and Yehuda Hellman, of the Conference of Presidents of Major American Jewish Organizations, and Isaiah M. Minkoff and Lewis H. Weinstein of the National Jewish Community Relations Advisory Council (NJCRAC), met to discuss the deteriorating conditions that were facing Soviet Jews. As a member of the executive board of President John F. Kennedy's Committee on Equal Opportunity in Housing, Weinstein was able to communicate to the president their concerns about these Jews and to get assurances that the matter would be broached to Premier Nikita Khrushchev. When the matter was mentioned to Khruschev, his response was not promising: "Mind your own business."[9]

In the meantime, the situation in the Soviet Union worsened. Synagogues were being forced to close (their number fell from 450 in 1956 to 96 in 1963), and Jews could no longer bury their dead in Jewish cemeteries. According to Dr. Israel Goldstein, who had recently travelled to Russia and other Iron Curtain countries, "Even within the general pattern of what is permitted by the regime to other religious groups, the Jewish religious group is not accorded equality of treatment." Individually, Russian Jews are treated with extraordinary cruelty.[10]

When Decter's conference was finally held, it issued a resolution that listed a voluminous "melancholy of persecution" that was being waged against the three million Jews in the Soviet Union, including Jewish youth being "deprived of . . . the most meager opportunities to acquire a knowledge of their Jewish heritage," the closing of "hundreds of synagogues" and the banning of private prayer meetings, and circumcision "largely abandoned through fear of censure and punishment."

In this way, "an ancient and illustrious community" was being "ground down, its spirit and consciousness pulverized." With Soviet Jews "helpless, defenseless and without voice," they had to rely on others to "do for them what they cannot do for themselves: We must ask for justice. We appeal for the redress of wrongs and for the restoration of rights.[11]

Among those signing the resolution were novelist Robert Penn Warren, Supreme Court Justice William O. Douglas, United Auto Worker union chief Walter Reuther, New York Senator Herbert H. Lehman—and Martin Luther King, Jr.

President Kennedy promised to pursue the matter after he returned from a trip to Dallas. But his assassination there on November 22 suspended any action from the White House. It would take another five months before Lyndon Johnson, in April 1964, became the first American president since Theodore Roosevelt to denounce Russian treatment of Jews.[12]

In late December 1963, however, Heschel wrote to the National Jewish Community Relations Advisory Council that unless it took some action to publicize the Soviet treatment of Jews, he would create a national organization to do just that:

> A person cannot be religious and indifferent to other human beings' plight and suffering. In fact, the tragedy of man is that so much of our history is a history of indifference dominated by a famous statement, Am I my brother's keeper?
>
> We are involved in the great battle for equal rights being waged in our country, and this great and victorious drama has electrified many millions of Americans. But another drama is being enacted which is agonizing, heartrending, tragic and ignored: the plight of the Jews in Soviet Russia.
>
> The essence of a Jew is his involvement in the plight of other people, as God is involved. This is the secret of our legacy . . . How can I call myself a Jew and remain indifferent to the spiritual extinction of so many Jews? . . .
>
> Prejudice is like a hydra, a monster which has many heads, an evil which requires many efforts to overcome. One head sends forth

poison against the people of a different race, another against people of a different religion or culture. . . .

We live in the darkest century of Jewish history. . . . Six million Jews are no more, and three million Jews are in the process of systematic spiritual liquidation. Those who really sense it live in dismay, while the majority of Jews in America don't even know about it and are at best indifferent. . . .

It is a burning sin that we remain indifferent. What is happening in our own days in America proves beyond doubt that a strong voice, ringing with force and dignity, has the power to pierce the iron shield of dormant conscience. We will get support from the Protestant and Catholic leadership, from the Negro leadership, in our effort to help save the Russian Jews from complete extinction.

What is called for is not a silent sigh but a voice of moral compassion and indignation, the sublime and inspired screaming of a prophet uttered by a whole community.

The Negro problem, I believe, is on the way to a solution because of the decision of the Supreme Court. Spirit has power. The voice of justice is stronger than bigotry. Yet, if not for personal involvement, if not for action on the part of the Negroes, the decision of the Supreme Court would have remained a still small voice, and the hour calls for the voice of justice as well as for concerted and incessant action.[13]

At a special President's Conference of Jewish Organizations meeting in mid-February, Heschel spoke about the need to speedily act on behalf of Soviet Jewry. The conference voted unanimously to adopt his proposal, and the America Jewish Committee agreed to participate. Together, they created the American Jewish Conference of Soviet Jewry.[14]

But not all Jewish groups were so receptive. Dr. Nahum Goldmann of the World Jewish Congress wrote from Geneva that American Jewish intervention in Soviet affairs would be troublesome: "I am sure that if Khrushchev would announce that he has officially received a delegation of Negroes in the Soviet Union to discuss the treatment of Negroes in the USA there would be an outcry of public opinion in America which would do the greatest harm to Soviet-American relations."[15]

Nevertheless, plans were made for a conference on Soviet Jewry to be held in Washington, D.C. in April. King, who was invited to participate, responded that he was "deeply in accord with what Rabbi Heschel has said concerning the injustices, the indignities and all of the humiliating experiences" that Soviet Jews were suffering. This attempt "to liquidate" Soviet Jews, to commit a "spiritual annihilation" must be prevented since "injustice anywhere is a threat to justice everywhere. Injustice to any people is a threat to justice to all people—and I cannot stand idly by, even though I live in the United States and even though I happen to be an American Negro, and fail to be concerned about what happens to my brothers and sisters who happen to be Jews in Soviet Russia. For what happens to them, happens to me—and to you; and we must be concerned.[16]

By January 14, 1965, the struggle for Soviet Jewry had become a national movement. An ad that day in the *New York Times*, "An Appeal to Conscience" organized by Rabbi Arthur Schneier of New York and protesting the harassment, staging of show-trials, and openly discriminatory behavior against Soviet Jews, was signed by a Who's Who of Americans. King added his name two days later:

> I am profoundly shocked by the treatment of the Jewish people in the Soviet Union. . . . I should like to add my voice to the list of distinguished Americans of all faiths who have called the injustices perpetrated against the Jewish community in the Soviet Union to the attention of the world. The struggle of the Negro people for freedom is inextricably interwoven with the universal struggle of all people to be free from discrimination and oppression. The Jewish people must be given their full rights as Soviet citizens as guaranteed by the Constitution of the USSR itself.

> The anti-Jewish tone of the economic trials must cease. The free functioning of synagogues should be permitted. There should be no interference with the performance of sacred rites. The religious and cultural freedom of this old Jewish community should be re-established.
>
> In the name of humanity, I urge that the Soviet government end all the discriminatory measures against its Jewish community. I will not remain silent in the face of injustice.[17]

On May 20, 1965, while receiving the American Civil Liberties Medallion from the American Jewish Committee, King encouraged "people all over the world" to engage "in mass action to protest anti-Semitism in the Soviet Union. There is a danger of silence today which unintentionally encourages evil to flourish. Albert Einstein was right when he said, "The world is in greater peril from those who tolerate evil than from those who actively commit it.""[18]

On June 3, a huge Soviet Jewry rally was held at Madison Square Garden in New York. Though he couldn't attend the rally, King sent his message of support of Soviet Jewry: "We in the civil rights movement have repeatedly made clear our commitment to the freedom of all men regardless of color, race, or creed. In light of this principle we deplore anti-Semitism as we deplore discrimination and segregation in Mississippi and Alabama."[19]

Bayard Rustin did attend the rally and soon expressed black leaders' commitment to Soviet Jews. At a vigil for Soviet Jews organized by the American Conference on Soviet Jewry, he told the ten thousand attendees that King and A. Philip Randolph had asked him to voice blacks' solidarity with Jewish religious and cultural freedom in Russia and throughout the world.[20]

This theme would be continued by other black leaders. Roy Wilkins, for instance, the executive director of the NAACP, drew parallels between blacks' struggle in the United States and Jews' struggle in the Soviet Union, since no matter where in the world injustice is done, justice everywhere is threatened; whenever injustice anywhere goes unchallenged, the cause of justice everywhere is prejudiced. Thus the struggle that the American Negro is waging—with much help from many American Jews for equality, for dignity, for a fair share in our society—that struggle is identified with the universal struggle of oppressed peoples for freedom.

. . . The Russian Government cannot put us off with stories about how happy Jews are in the Soviet Union, with pictures of crowded synagogues on High Holy Days, or with protestations by Party Jews who are lackeys to the regime. We have heard too many stories about how content Negroes were under the Deep South system. We've had too many Uncle Toms. And we have learned in recent years what lies behind the mask, once the prospect of freedom is raised and the oppressor can be challenged openly.

Nor can the Soviet Government put us off with small grudging concessions: a few pounds of *matzo* for Passover, an occasional Yiddish book of verse, a casual pro forma denunciation of anti-Semitism. We American Negroes have seen too much tokenism here at home to be impressed by it abroad.

What is there to do? There is this to do—rouse the conscience of the world, demand again and again, and louder and louder until the voices of indignation and protest penetrate the Iron Curtain and the stone walls of the Kremlin and the minds of the Soviet leaders—demand that the Jews of Russia be accorded the full and equal rights of Soviet citizens.

Soviet Jews themselves cannot participate in this appeal to the conscience of the world. But we shall be their voice. All of us, regardless of race, color, nativity, or religion, must be their voice, as Americans always have been when a cry for deliverance has reached our land. And we will prevail.[21]

For December 1966, a national Soviet Jewry Human Rights Day was planned, with King invited to participate because, as he was told, his voice would command the attention of all who were committed to the protection of human rights.

King accepted. He spoke on a telephone hookup to twelve sites around the country, cautioning that "no person of good will can stand by as a silent auditor while there is a possibility of the complete spiritual and cultural destruction of a once-flourishing Jewish community. The denial of human rights anywhere is a threat to the affirmation of human rights everywhere."

Jews in Russia, he continued,

> may not be physically murdered as they were in Nazi Germany, [but] they are facing every day a kind of spiritual and cultural genocide. Individual Jews may in the main be physically and economically secure in Russia, but the absence of opportunity to associate as Jews in the enjoyment of Jewish culture and religious experience becomes a severe limitation upon the individual. These deprivations are a part of a person's emotional and intellectual life. They determine whether he is fulfilled as a human being. Negroes can well understand and sympathize with this problem. When you are written out of history as a people, when you are given no choice but to accept the majority culture, you are denied an aspect of your own identity. Ultimately you suffer a corrosion of your self-understanding and your self-respect. . . .
>
> World public opinion is justified in reminding . . . [the Soviets] that they are repressing a cultural heritage that is world property. Jewish history and culture are a part of everyone's heritage, whether he be Jewish, Christian or Moslem. The Soviet Union must recognize the legitimate criticism that insists it accord fair treatment to its Jewish community. If that government expects respect for itself in the international community of nations, the sincere and genuine concern felt by so many people around the world for this problem should impel the Soviet government not only to effect a solution but to do so with all deliberate speed. In the meantime, let us continue to make our voices heard and our righteous protests felt. We cannot sit complacently by the wayside while our Jewish brothers in the Soviet Union face the possible extinction of their cultural and spiritual life. Those that sit at rest, while others take pains, are tender turtles and buy their quiet with disgrace.[22]

It would take many more years before the Soviet repression of Jews would abate. With perestroika and the premiership of Mikhail Gorbachev in the 1980s, the situation of Jewish people in the USSR relaxed, and they could practice their religion and open religious schools and rabbinic seminaries. Hundreds of thousands emigrated, mostly to the United States and Israel. Lost in the flush of success and the fog of memory were the indispensable contributions to the Soviet Jewry movement that had come from black leaders in the United States—especially Martin Luther King, Jr.—who already had more than a full-time commitment to their own movement, but who saw in Soviet Jews a situation so similar to theirs in the United States that they knew they could not remain silent.

13

A Poisoned Fountain: St. Augustine

The city of St. Augustine, Florida, founded by the Spanish in 1565, is the oldest city in the United States. The explorer Ponce de Leon landed in the area in 1513 during his search for the legendary fountain of Youth. It is dedicated to tourism, as are so many other Florida towns, and was first promoted for travelers from the north by railroad magnate Henry Flagler in the 1880s. In 1964, it was preparing to celebrate its quadricentennial. But the national headlines it reaped had nothing to do with St. Augustine as a tourist mecca or a historical landmark. Rather, they described St. Augustine as one of the most entrenched racist communities in the United States.

> According to a Negro dentist named Robert B. Hayling, elementary law had ceased to exist for the Negroes of St. Augustine. . . . Here Sheriff L. O. Davis . . . employed an auxiliary force of one hundred deputies, many of them prominent Klansmen, to "keep the niggers in line." Here barrel-chested Holsted "Hoss" Manucy, dressed in cowboy

paraphernalia, led a bunch of Klan-style bullyboys who called themselves the Ancient City Gun Club. They patrolled the county in radio
cars with Confederate flags on their antennas, harassing Negroes at
will. Manucy boasted that he had no vices, that he didn't smoke, drink,
or chase women. All he did was "beat and kill niggers."[1]

Hayling, an Air Force veteran who would not readily submit to
second-class citizenship, had tried for years to unite St. Augustine's
blacks against racial discrimination and the terror tactics perpetrated
by the white hoodlums retained by the town to keep blacks in their
place. Despite cross-burnings and threats of physical violence, he
persisted in his efforts, even traveling to Washington to ask for federal assistance. In retaliation, in September of 1963, he was kidnapped
by Klansmen. In an open field, with three others, Hayling was beat-
en with brass knuckles and ax handles. Only the sheriff's arrival prevented the mob from pouring kerosene on him and lighting a match.
Then, in February 1964, his house was shot at. His dog was killed,
and his wife and children barely escaped injury. Unaware of what
was happening at home, he was at his office protecting it from threatened arson.[2]

Hayling had no help from the NAACP—his brusque arrogance
had already alienated the local chapter—or from federal authorities.
So he turned to the SCLC.

Rev. C. T. Vivian, the SCLC's director of affiliates and one of the
earliest Freedom Riders, soon visited St. Augustine and reported back
to Hayling that the SCLC could provide him with little assistance.
With no full-scale backing from St. Augustine's blacks, the SCLC
would not engage in another debacle similar to what had happened
in Albany, Georgia. Until the community formed its own leadership
around which it could rally, the SCLC could offer only guidance, not
the money and manpower for a campaign. Least of all could it provide the presence of Martin Luther King, Jr.

With Vivian's assistance, Hayling formed a local SCLC chapter and started asking Northern clergy to witness the horrors of St. Augustine and lend their moral support to the struggle of the city's blacks. The SCLC's Hosea Williams also arrived to begin organizing for a campaign.

For the fewer than fifty families who made up St. Augustine's Jewish community, these were perilous times. If any of them said anything in favor of black rights, they could easily find themselves facing Hoss Manucy's cattle prod–bearing sadists. Few of them could openly agree with the feelings expressed about the situation in St. Augustine by Rabbi William Silverman of Nashville, Tennessee:

> If we are to be true to our heritage of prophetic Judaism, . . . every congregation must stand and be counted. We should live by our faith and implement the moral ideals of social justice taught to us by the prophets of Israel. Much more is involved than attacks upon the Negro. The Negro is the initial target in the mobilization of the bigots for warfare against moral and spiritual values. The ultimate objective is to attack the principles and precepts of the Judeo-Christian way of life. There is a time when silence is cowardly. There is a time when our faith must commit us to moral action. Now is such a time.[3]

But in St. Augustine, where fear of economic or physical reprisals were rampant, all a Jew could do was philosophize, which is what many other Southern Jews and liberal Southerners were already doing. As scholar Henry Baron had told St. Louis' Jewish Community Relations Council just two years before:

> [T]he Southern Jew generally is more keenly aware of the special character his Jewishness gives him than is his co-religionist in the North. Jews in New York, Chicago, or Boston live among a host of religious, ethnic, and racial groups, none of which can claim majority status. But in most Southern communities the very small number of

Jewish families are an obvious minority in an otherwise homogeneous white Protestant society. Their contacts with Christians are cordial, but rarely extend beyond business hours or community service efforts.

These factors help shape Southern Jews' contradictory attitudes on the race question. Most Jews probably feel a natural sympathy for the aspirations of the Negroes, whom they see as a minority group now journeying down something like the same road they had to travel. But they are unwilling to set themselves off from the dominant white majority, to which they have made such strenuous efforts to belong. So they generally keep their views to themselves—which causes further uneasiness. Because the thoughts they harbor on the race issue may differ from those of the majority of their white neighbors, they may feel "disloyal" to Southern attitudes and institutions.[4]

But there was a distinction between Southern attitudes and Northern attitudes, and the SCLC's Massachusetts office began a concerted effort to bring protestors to St. Augustine. Among those arrested for violating Florida's "undesirable visitor and trespass" laws was Mary Peabody, the mother of the governor of Massachusetts. She was also the wife of Episcopal Bishop Malcolm Peabody and the cousin of Eleanor Roosevelt. Her arrest brought national headlines.

William Kunstler, who had become, essentially, a "movement lawyer," was recruited in a midnight phone call to defend Peabody. He later remembered that all the lawyers for the defendants "immediately jumped up and objected" when St. Augustine's lawyers addressed the single black witness—fifteen-year-old Annie Evans—by her first name: the Supreme Court had recently ruled that blacks addressed in court by their first names were not required to answer questions. When the judge directed the city's counsel to revise his language, he properly addressed her as "Miss Evans."

"It was a great moment," he recalled, "one of those that I live for in the courtroom. She lit up with a huge smile; the respect automatically given to white witnesses had finally, and rightly been given to young Annie Evans."[5]

In the meantime, SCLC's Hosea Williams began pushing for night marches to St. Augustine's Slave Market. This was an open invitation for violence. On May 28, as Andrew Young led a column of marchers, they were set upon by Klansmen wielding chains and iron pipes. Local police looked on while Young was beaten unconscious. Newspapers and television stations ran pictures of the beating. On May 31, King arrived on the scene. By June 9, he was in jail, having demanded service in a local segregated restaurant. While he was in prison, four hundred black individuals were attacked by a white mob.

Upon his release, a haggard King flew to Yale to receive an honorary degree. But he quickly returned. While in jail he had written to his old friend, Rabbi Israel Dresner, about bringing a group of rabbis to St. Augustine. As Dresner gathered rabbis who were ready to depart for St. Augustine, J. B. Stoner, the vice-presidential candidate of the National States' Rights Party, arrived in the city to add his own brand of incendiary dialogue to the fray.

The demonstrations in St. Augustine resumed. Every day, marchers walked to the site of the city's Slave Market. King, who was living in a rented house on the beach, was luckily not home when gunshots ripped into the walls of his cabin.

When local police ordered the marches to cease, Kunstler requested a federal injunction against city officials. He presented his arguments in the Jacksonville federal court before "a tall, stately" judge "who liked to whittle with his penknife while he was on the bench." The petition claimed that the marches had been peaceful and that any violence had been caused by police and white counterdemonstrators. On June 9, a federal judge ordered St. Augustine officials not to interfere with the marches. With that, according to Kunstler, "all hell broke loose. When blacks attempted to use the St. Augustine beaches, the sand was bloodied as a result of violence instigated by white counter-demonstrators and police. Although the federal court had previously ordered St. Augustine to integrate, the ingrained racism in that city made it almost impossible for the city's black residents to benefit from the court order. The violence by whites was incredible, and mob rule by bands of Klan members and other thugs wreaked havoc on blacks and those whites who stood by them."[6]

The Central Conference of American Rabbis (CCAR), the national organization of Reform rabbis, was then holding its national convention in Atlantic City. King sent a telegram for them to join him in St. Augustine. Of the hundreds of rabbis in attendance, only sixteen—and Albert Vorspan, the CCAR's lay administrator—went to St. Augustine. Rabbi Arnold Jacob Wolf, a leading social activist, explained this minimal response, since he, also, remained at the convention:

> I must ask myself what the meaning of my refusal to answer Dr. King's call was, a refusal shared by nearly all my colleagues on this and nearly every other occasion. . . . The real reason for my refusal . . . is more than the sum of my personal inadequacies . . . [and] wider than the total anxiety of the community. . . . When I said no, I meant it. No—I do not really wish to work with you! I do not wish to swim with you! I do not wish to go to jail with you! I do not wish to eat your food or be one of you!
>
>   . . . As an American rabbi, I am inevitably and incurably bourgeois. . . . The American Jew lives by his superiority to and distance from the American Negro and the American poor. And I live off him! Both of us are terribly frightened by the new American Revolution. Like most revolutions in the past, this one is likely to do the Jew no "good."[7]

Among the rabbis who did go were Eugene Borowitz, Balfour Brickner, Israel Dresner, Jerold Goldstein, Joel S. Goor, Richard Levy, Eugene Lipman, B. T. Rubinstein and Allen Secher. When they arrived on June 17 at the church in St. Augustine where the marchers were having a rally, King

> announced their entrance to an enthusiastic crowd, then invited . . . Dresner to speak from the pulpit. Dresner, as the only Reform volunteer with experience at such events, astonished his colleagues with call-and-response preaching that evoked a tumultuous response. Carried away, he retained his customary long-windedness beyond the endurance of several rabbis who, wilting from fatigue in the Florida heat, discreetly chanted *genug*—Yiddish for "enough already." They all followed . . . Andrew Young on a long march beyond the Slave Market, then dispersed for the night in Negro homes as King debated strategy. Judaism, King said, had given the world that love of freedom which now inspired the Negro Revolution and "now these rabbis have come here to stand by our side, to witness to our common convictions."[8]

Rabbi Secher never forgot that nighttime march through St. Augustine:

> We formed a line to do the march, our pockets emptied so there would be no suggestion we bore weapons, and as things would happen, I was paired with a black woman first in line. A couple of hundred people, we marched through the same area where the night before someone had been shot. Here I was walking with a black woman singing freedom songs and walking down dark streets. Courage is horsefeathers. Scared is real. But I knew that this is where I had to be, to do the right thing.[9]

Surprisingly, state troopers were on the scene, and everything was shut down tight for the night. There was no trouble. The next day, the rabbis met again with King in the church, then starting marching to the segregated Monson's Motor Lodge. But this new march, as Vorspan wrote, was

> under the noonday sun—and this time we saw the faces of the "enemy." I was shocked to realize that my anxiety was not much different, though more acute, than what I used to feel when, on occasion, I walked through Harlem at night. Implacable hatred stabbed out at us from old men, women and young people alike lining the sidewalks. There was murder in those faces.[10]

As the marchers approached the motor lodge, the owner, James Brock, promptly had them arrested for trespassing. In front of reporters and television cameramen, fifteen rabbis and other demonstrators were jammed into police cars and hauled away.

Kunstler recalled another salient event that occurred that same day:

> Fred Shuttlesworth led a group of blacks and whites to the dining room of the Monson Motel. They were ejected by the manager, who was too busy arguing with them to notice that seven people—two whites and five blacks—were in the motel's pool. The manager responded to this by pouring muriatic acid into the water and calling in police to arrest the swimmers.[11]

When Vorspan and Borowitz entered the motel with several blacks, Brock, the owner, begged them not to force him to have them arrested. "Look," responded Borowitz, "we did not come here to create trouble for you, but only to ask you to do what you know in your heart is right." "I wish I could," he sighed, "but I can't." Brock had them arrested.[12]

At the jail, they met the infamous Hoss Manucy, the majordomo of St. Augustine's jail, who sneered at them, "Cain't figger out why you white nigger rabbis mixed yourself up in this thing. Why, our niggers was getting' along just fine. . . . Oh yes. We have a real good Jew lawyer in town here, and he tells me that you ain't Jews at all. You're kikes, that's what you are."[13]

When word of the rabbis' arrest reached the CCAR convention in Atlantic City, an announcement was made of their plight and "our prayers and best wishes and our sense of gratitude" were extended.[14] Even if the rabbis had known of the conference's good wishes, it would have done little to ameliorate their situation.

[P]arched and miserable [in jail] after sun-drenched hours in the outdoor "chicken coop," the prisoners refused an order to come inside to segregated cells. While guards fetched Sheriff Davis, the rabbis formed a protective circle around Shuttlesworth and Vivian, vowing to stand on their constitutional right to remain together with the Negro clergy. Shuttlesworth laughed, saying they did not understand jails, but the rabbis held firm through booming threats and pointed guns until Sheriff Davis had a Negro teenager hauled from the cell block and shocked in front of them with a cattle prod, causing her to scream and shrivel to the floor like an autumn leaf. Then they parted to let the Negro prisoners separate, and marveled when Shuttlesworth veered toward Sheriff Davis to say, "I love you, brother."[15]

The rabbis were treated little better than the blacks. They "had to run the gauntlet of state troopers," which was "like running gauntlets of Nazis. They weren't there to protect us; they vilified us as we went, restraining themselves from beating us. We were outsiders, troublemakers, we were the problem, and they really wanted to beat us. Hoss Manucy would have liked to string us up, but the media was all over the place. But he did use cattle prods on us."[16]

But once they got past the gauntlet and the cattle prods and could think more clearly and with slightly less fear, the rabbis talked in their cells "until dawn about what had brought them from eight different states to such a place. . . . One by one, with Borowitz taking notes on the back of a leaflet about the Ku Klux Klan, each man spoke, and then they composed a lengthy common testament . . . 'We shall not forget the people with whom we drove, prayed, marched, slept, ate, demonstrated and were arrested. How little we know of these people and their struggle. . . . How many a Torah reading, Passover celebration, prayer book text and sermonic effort has come to mind in these hours.' . . . These words were first written at 3:00 A.M. in . . . sweltering heat, . . . by the light of the one naked bulb hanging in the corridor outside . . . [our] small cell."[17]

The next day, a representative of the local Jewish community visited the rabbis. Instead of words of fellowship, he derided them for coming to town, telling them all they had accomplished was to foment anti-Semitism. As Rabbi Goor later noted, "The one local Jew who visited us in prison came not to comfort us but to show the jailer that he was a "'White Jew.'"[18]

On Friday, most of the rabbis refused their first jail food—small jars of Gerber's Baby Food merrily offered as a "special meal"—and were bailed out to fly home for the Sabbath. Shortly after the rabbis' departure came the announcement that the Senate had passed the Civil Rights Act for which King had so long fought. When St. Augustine learned that the bill had been enacted, Stone and Hoss Manucy raged that it would "bring on a race war" and whipped a thousand whites into an anti-Negro frenzy. On the night of June 25, eight hundred club-wielding Klansmen moved out of the Slave Market and slashed through a silent column of blacks who were marching through the square. A white journalist reported that "the mob emitted an eerie cry as it crossed and recrossed the plaza," clubbing Negroes to the pavement, ripping the clothes off a thirteen-year-old girl, and mauling a female reporter from *Newsweek* until the journalist intervened and helped her escape.[19]

Though the situation was out of control, state authorities and federal marshals provided no help. Finally, Judge Simpson intervened with the help of the governor. Together, they established an emergency biracial committee composed of the polarized factions of St. Augustine. That was sufficient for King to order the marchers to cease. "Every thousand-mile journey begins with the first step," he said. "This is merely the first step in the long journey toward freedom and justice in St. Augustine." King knew well that St. Augustine would not be desegregated without more bloodshed, but he wanted to pause to see what would happen next.

Days later, on the Fourth of July, President Johnson signed into law the Civil Rights Act of 1964. The new law integrated all public accommodations in the United States. It was a direct result of the civil rights protests and demonstrations in the South, and it helped end overt segregation in St. Augustine—and everywhere else.[20]

Vorspan now reflects that "King was the only person in the country for whom we would have signed a blank check. And our participation in St. Augustine was a blank check. We didn't know what was going to happen to us, but none of us ever felt that we had been entrapped. We walked into it with open eyes."[21]

But still, three decades later, Vorspan has never returned to the oldest city in the United States.

14

A Kindred Spirit:
Abraham Joshua Heschel

Abraham Joshua Heschel once wrote that the Hebrew Bible "is not a history of the Jewish people but the story of God's quest for the righteous man." Because of "the failure" of the human race as a whole to be righteous, Jews feel it is individuals, such as Noah or Abraham, or a remnant of a people, such as the Jews, whose task is "to satisfy that quest by making every man a righteous man."[1]

Many people would include Abraham Joshua Heschel among the righteous of the twentieth century. A religious scholar, a social activist, a teacher, a prophet, Heschel was willing to step forward, to put himself on the line, to challenge the establishment and challenge himself. And, in an act of what seemed to be divine intervention, he would meet and become friends with a kindred spirit, a man who held similar beliefs and love of God—Martin Luther King, Jr. The strength of that bond, and their common concern for social justice, led one historian to conclude that while King was "the architect of the nonviolent civil rights movement . . . Heschel was its Jewish conscience."[2]

King and Heschel came together from wildly divergent worlds; yet, they shared a common philosophy and common goals. Heschel's words were uniquely his, but they embodied and reflected the mission that was also uniquely King's:

> The way we act, the way we fail to act is a disgrace which must not go on forever. This is not a white man's world. This is not a colored man's world. It is God's world. No man has a place in this world who tries to keep another man in his place. It is time for the white man to repent. We have failed to use the avenues open to us to educate the hearts and minds of men, to identify ourselves with those who are underprivileged. But repentance is more than contrition and remorse for sins, for harms done. Repentance means a new insight, a new spirit. It also means a course of action.[3]

Heschel was born in Warsaw, Poland, in 1907. His family of renowned Hasidic scholars soon discovered it had an intellectual prodigy on its hands when he received *smicha* (rabbinic ordination) while still in his teens. At the University of Berlin, he would publish a collection of Yiddish poetry, a work on Maimonides, and a dissertation on the biblical prophets.

In 1938, the Gestapo deported Heschel to Poland. He managed to flee to England and, in 1940, was offered a teaching position at Hebrew Union College (HUC) in Cincinnati. Though HUC, as a Reform Jewish institution, was markedly different from the Orthodox tradition in which he had been raised, he accepted the post.

Heschel never returned to the land of his birth, where much of his family had been killed during the Holocaust. "If I should go to Poland or Germany," he explained, "every stone, every tree would remind me of contempt, hatred, murder, of children killed, of mothers burned alive, of human beings asphyxiated."[4]

He soon moved to The Jewish Theological Seminary of America, the Conservative movement's seminary in New York.

Although it was closer to his Orthodox roots than HUC had been, this was still not an easy fit for him. It was rumored that one of the reasons he had been hired was to serve as "an ornament of piety," that he could discourage criticism that the seminary was "a haven for Reconstructionist teachers who held that atheism was an acceptable, even preferred, belief for rabbinical students." Heschel was not allowed to teach courses on Jewish philosophy or theology, the very subjects that had helped make his reputation in Berlin and Frankfurt before his departure from Germany. One biographer has written that he "bridled at the constraints [under which he labored at the New York seminary]. Students were startled to hear him say they were being trained for mere synagogue administration in the guise of the rabbinate, as it was possible to complete the seminary curriculum without attending a single class on the Jewish conception of God."[5]

Though grateful for having been saved from the Hitler's Europe, Heschel still rankled at his situation. One of his aphorisms may have hit very close to home: "Disparity between man's appearance and reality is a condition of social integration. Suppressions are the price he pays for being accepted in society. Adjustment involves assenting to odd auspices, concessions of conscience, inevitable hypocrisies. It is, indeed, often a life of 'quiet desperation.'"[6]

But Heschel was not the sort of person who would be content living a life of "quiet desperation." As his proficiency with English grew, he published books of aphorisms that received positive public acceptance by Jew and Gentile alike. One of these advised that,

A MORAL PERSON is a partisan who loves the love of good. It is not true that love and obedience cannot live together, that the good never springs from the heart. To be free of selfish interests does not mean to be neutral, indifferent, or devoid of interests, but, on the contrary, to be a partisan of the self-surpassing. God does not dwell beyond the sky. He dwells, we believe, in every heart that is willing to let Him in.[7]

In 1961, as his fame was growing, Heschel began quietly lobbying Vatican II (the Ecumenical Council called by Pope John XXIII) to address the issue of anti-Semitism. His efforts began the process that would culminate in the council absolving Jews of the charge of murdering Jesus. This was an intense, often difficult reassessment of age-old anti-Semitic teachings. Though for years his role was kept under wraps, by the mid-1960s, after a visit to Pope Paul VI, knowledge of his efforts became known.

In the meantime, Heschel decided to translate into English his German dissertation on the biblical prophets. In the process of preparing this work, he became moved by the moral courage of these men of the past who had challenged the status quo of their age. Convinced of the need to be more of an activist in human affairs himself, Heschel accepted an invitation from a Detroit rabbi, Morris Adler, to attend a conference on religion and race that he was organizing for the National Conference of Christians and Jews. At the conference, which was held in Chicago in January 1963, Heschel wryly observed that "at the first conference on religion and race, the main participants . . . [had been] Pharaoh and Moses. Moses' words were: Thus saith the Lord, the God of Israel, Let My people go that they may celebrate a feast unto Me. While Pharaoh retorted: Who is the Lord, that I should heed His voice and let Israel go? I do not know the Lord, and moreover I will not let Israel go."[8]

> The outcome of that summit meeting has not come to an end. Pharaoh is not ready to capitulate.... In fact, it was easier for the children of Israel to cross the Red Sea than for a Negro to cross certain university campuses. Religion and race. How can the two be uttered together? To act in the spirit of religion is to unite what lies apart, to remember that humanity as a whole is God's beloved child. To act in the spirit of race is to sunder, to slash, to dismember the flesh of living humanity. How can we hear the word "race" and feel no self-

reproach? Racism is worse than idolatry. Racism is satanism. Few of us seem to realize how insidious, how radical, how universal and evil, racism is. Few of us realize that racism is man's gravest threat to man ... Race prejudice is a treacherous denial of the existence of God. Faith in God is not simply an afterlife-insurance policy. Racial or religious bigotry must be recognized for what it is: atheism.... Prayer and prejudice cannot dwell in the same heart.[9]

The conference provided the first meeting between Heschel and King, who also spoke in Chicago. That encounter developed into a life-long friendship and intellectual bond. Moreover, the two men raised strikingly similar cries. Each quoted the prophet Amos: "Let justice roll down like waters, and righteousness like a mighty stream." Both quoted theologian Reinhold Niebuhr. And both understood that the sins of racism demanded the fierce and compassionate presence of prophets who could, as Heschel's daughter, Susannah, later wrote, "draw upon themselves the excess poison in the world. . . . [King and Heschel's] communion on this rich subject was a pleasant surprise to both men, who vowed to see more of each other; and for once King encountered an orator who reached for notes in his register. 'Let there be a grain of prophet in every man!' Heschel exclaimed."[10]

Years later, Heschel's daughter examined the philosophical bond that had brought these two men together:

The preference King gives to the Exodus motif over the figure of Jesus certainly played a major role in linking the two men intellectually and religiously; for Heschel, the primacy of the Exodus in the civil rights movement was a major step in the history of Christian-Jewish relations. King's understanding of the nature of God's involvement with humanity, derived from the black church, bears striking similarities to Heschel's concept of divine pathos and provided the basis of the spiritual affinity they felt for each other ... nurtured by the surprising spiritual connections informing their understandings of the Bible.[11]

But it was in the biblical pronouncements of the prophets that the thinking of these two men especially merged. Both catapulted the questions of the day into a biblical template: they occur not only on a human plane but within the life of God as well. Heschel placed this in a tradition that was well established within Jewish mysticism. And King, by equating what was occurring in, say, Alabama with the Exodus was engaged in more than a politically astute use of a biblical story but in an effort to place the participants in the civil rights struggle in the biblical realm—a realm in which actions have consequences for the divine plan of history.

The two men also shared a fundamental assumption that there was a divine concern with civil rights.

God, too, was involved with the struggle because God was not remote but was affected by how humans treated one another.

Fulfilling his new-found dedication to social activism, Heschel decided to demonstrate against the plight of Soviet Jewry. In August 1962, he declared: "The voice of our brother's agony is crying to us! How can we be silent? How can we remain passive? How can we have peace of mind or live with our conscience?"[12]

Fourteen months later, in November 1963, King and Heschel again shared a podium, this time at the biannual convention of the United Synagogue of America, the Conservative Movement's congregational organization, held at the sprawling Concord Hotel in Kiamesha Lake, New York. Heschel introduced King and presented him with the United Synagogue's Solomon Schechter Award. And King, as Taylor Branch later wrote, "praised Heschel for following the prophets' example of speaking the harshest truths to the closest kin—in this case, for saying that even Jews managed indifference to slow spiritual liquidation under Communism." The next day at the annual convention of Reform congregations, which was being held in Chicago, King condemned the plight of Soviet Jews. He was "happy" to see placards urging Protestants, Catholics, and Jews to join together to aid Jews in the USSR. Denouncing the "systematic attempt" to eradicate Judaism in the Soviet Union, he ensured the audience that "men of good will will not allow it to take place. . . . I cannot stand idly by as an American Negro and not be concerned about what happens to my brothers and sisters who happen to be Jews in Soviet Russia. For their problem is my problem."[13]

Over the next few years, King and Heschel appeared together on many occasions, the most prominent of which was the Selma-to-Montgomery March in 1965. Before going to Selma, Heschel had organized eight hundred demonstrators who converged on the FBI headquarters in New York to protest the treatment of the demonstrators who were already marching in Selma. Only Heschel was allowed inside the building to present a petition decrying the lack of federal assistance in guaranteeing the Selma participants their civil rights. A few days later, on a Friday afternoon, a telegram came from King asking Heschel to join him in Selma. In the Heschel household, as Susannah Heschel recalled,

There was a flurry of activity, arranging of flights and packing, before the Sabbath began. When it became dark on Saturday and the Sabbath ended, we went downstairs to see my father off. I remember kissing him goodbye, watching him get into the yellow Checker cab and drive off, and wondering if I would ever see him again. Both my mother and I worried terribly the next days. Demonstrations in the South at that time were fierce and dangerous. We used to see Sheriff Bull Connor of Birmingham, Alabama, on the television news, unleashing dogs and aiming water hoses at demonstrators. My father was not young and not able to protect himself physically."[14]

In Selma, wearing a lei that a contingent of Hawaiian supporters had given him, Heschel found himself at the head of the march with King and another Nobel laureate, Ralph Bunche. With his head of white hair and white beard, Heschel—"Father Abraham," as civil rights workers called him, and "my rabbi" as King called him— looked like a true biblical prophet facing down the angry crowds of Alabama.

When he finally came home, Heschel's wife and daughter were "relieved and proud," and Susannah's math teacher, the only black teacher in her school, took her aside and told her what a wonderful thing her father had done. Later, Heschel told her how he had experienced the march: "I felt my legs were praying."[15]

"For my father," Susannah later wrote,

> the march was a religious moment. He wrote in his memoir: "I thought of my having walked with Hasidic rabbis on various occasions. I felt a sense of the Holy in what I was doing...." With sadness, my father added, "I felt again what I have been thinking about for years—that Jewish religious institutions have again missed a great opportunity, namely, to interpret a civil-rights movement in terms of Judaism. The vast number of Jews participating actively in it are totally unaware of what the movement means in terms of the prophetic traditions."[16]

Soon after the march, Heschel invited King to a Passover service at his home in New York. Unfortunately, King did not attend the seder. But one Saturday night in 1966, just prior to *havdalah*, the lighting of a special candle at the conclusion of the Sabbath, there was a knock on Heschel's door. There stood King and Rev. William Sloane Coffin, a Heschel friend who was also active in the civil rights and anti-Vietnam War movements. In a few minutes, the visitors were participating in the Sabbath ceremonies, with Coffin holding the traditional spice box and King holding the *havdalah* candle. Afterward, after lighting up the cigar he was rarely without, Heschel told them a traditional allegory that asked, "How does a person grow—from the head down or from the feet up?" But Heschel revised the story so it would address the notion of growth occurring from the inside out. Moses, for instance, said Heschel, had grown as a person when he took upon himself the mantle of his people. The reference could not be lost on anyone in that room—they were in the presence of a new Moses, one who had come from Georgia, not from the wilderness of Sinai.[17]

Two years later—March 25, 1968—King spoke at the annual convention of the Conservative movement's Rabbinical Assembly. As he entered the hall in a Catskills hotel he was greeted by a thousand rabbis singing "We Shall Overcome" in Hebrew. Heschel, who was celebrating his birthday, was on hand to introduce his friend to the assembly. King, he said, was "a voice, a vision, and a way," one whom every Jew and every American should listen to. He was an antidote to the "astute" politicians, the "proud" establishment, the "busy" market place: "Placid, happy, merry, the people pursue their work, enjoy their leisure, and life is fair; people buy, sell, celebrate and rejoice. They fail to realize that in the midst of our affluent cities there are districts of despair, areas of distress."

King, said Heschel, was a modern-day prophet; his voice was equal to that of the Prophets of Israel and his presence was "a sign that God has not forsaken the United States of America. God has sent him to us. His presence is the hope of America. His mission is sacred; his leadership of supreme importance to every one of us."[18]

King quickly reciprocated with praise for his friend:

> Over the last few years, being involved in the struggle for racial jus-
> tice, ... often I have seen religious leaders stand amid the social injus-
> tices that pervade our society, mouthing pious irrelevancies and
> sanctimonious trivialities. All too often the religious community has
> been a tail light instead of a head light. But here and there we find
> those who refuse to remain silent behind the safe security of stained

glass windows, and they are forever seeking to make the great ethical insights of our Judeo-Christian heritage relevant in this day and in this age.... Rabbi Heschel is one of the persons who is relevant at all times, always standing with prophetic insights to guide us through these difficult days.

He has been with us in many of our struggles. I remember marching from Selma to Montgomery, how he stood at my side and with us as we faced that crisis situation. I remember very well when we were in Chicago for the Conference on Religion and Race. Eloquently and profoundly, he spoke . . . and to a great extent this speech inspired clergymen of all the religious faiths of our country; many went out and decided to do something that they had not done before. So I am happy to be here with him, and I want to say Happy Birthday, and I hope I can be here to celebrate your one hundredth birthday.[19]

Like King, Heschel also opposed the Vietnam War. On April 4, 1967, both were on the podium at an anti-war rally in New York City at The Riverside Church. There, before rabbis and priests and ministers and anti-war protestors, King assailed the war as a corrupt distraction from the indispensable need to reform America at home, to attend to its poor and its cities and its own racial tensions and divisions. In some ways, he said, the war—white soldiers fighting Asian peasants—was a projection of the racial cancer that was plaguing America on its own shores.

King's speech antagonized members of the civil rights establishment who felt he was abandoning its constituency. It also disturbed major Jewish organizations: Though most disliked the war, they were extremely cautious in their public opposition to it, since President Johnson had warned them that any anti-war stands from them would jeopardize American support for Israel.

When King was killed a year later, Heschel deeply grieved. King, he said, "was one of the greatest prophetic spirits we had in this century. . . . He brought great blessing to the world—to all of us concerned with the rights of man."[20] Heschel traveled to King's funeral in Atlanta with SCLC workers Peter Geffen, a founder of New York's Heschel School, and Mickey Shur, who later became Rabbi Moshe Shur. Heschel was the only rabbi who delivered a eulogy. After the wake at the Ebenezer Baptist Church, the three men walked to the memorial services at Morehouse College and then back to Heschel's hotel. On the walk back, Geffen and Shur asked Heschel, "What do we do now?" Heschel responded, "You must teach the children, so they may remake the world."[21]

On December 23, 1972, Rabbi Abraham Joshua Heschel died of a heart attack, but not before he, too, had helped remake the world.

15

Selma: The Ultimate Freedom March

I n October 1964, after King received the Nobel Peace Prize for
his nonviolent approach to civil rights, a group of blacks asked Ralph
McGill, the publisher of the *Atlanta Constitution*, to help organize an
interracial testimonial dinner. McGill liked the idea and, with
Benjamin Mays, the president of Morehouse College, Archbishop
Paul J. Hallinan, and Rabbi Jacob Rothschild, called on Mayor Ivan
Allen. Allen immediately agreed with the proposal but didn't admit
the trepidation he felt:

> We still had more than our share of racists and bigots in Atlanta and
> the rest of the South, and not all of them were blue-collar Wallaceites
> living with their hatred and bitterness on the fringes of town. Many of
> these people made up the privileged Southern class: people who
> belong to the exclusive country clubs and work in air-conditioned sky-
> scrapers and go home every evening to expensive lily-white suburbs
> so they can carry on their tirade against the Negro in smug isolation.

There was still great bitterness inside the Southern business community toward Dr. King's successful efforts at desegregating public facilities. And so the awarding of the Nobel Peace Prize to him brought the haters out of the woodwork once more.[1]

Nevertheless, Mayor Allen persisted, twisting arms and getting the support of Robert W. Woodruff, the seventy-five-year-old president of Coca-Cola, the largest business in the city. With Woodruff on board, and after a New York Times article described the resistance within Atlanta's establishment to honoring King, the embarrassed Atlanta elite fell into line. Soon, the attitude "We ain't gonna have no dinner for no nigger"[2] gave way to a demand for tickets that far exceeded the available seating. As Rothschild recalled:

To have such a dinner in Atlanta, Georgia, in those days was not at all a simple, uncomplicated undertaking.... [King was a] controversial figure; the power structure and the politicians were not about to leap for joy at the prospect of honoring him. There were a few of us, however, who were determined that the city of his birth and his adult ministry would do just that.... A handful of us met for weeks making plans and arrangements without any hope of fulfilling them. And after all the foot-dragging and outright opposition, exactly 1,463 people gathered to honor Dr. King in the largest room then available [in Atlanta]. Another thousand were turned away. It was the largest gathering of whites and blacks—roughly two hundred more whites than Negroes—in the history of our city. We had to turn away for lack of space many of the most prominent of our citizens who leaped too late on the bandwagon."[3]

As chairman of the festivities, Rothschild opened the event with a resounding acknowledgment of those in attendance:

You attest the truth that goodness and righteousness do reside in the human heart. You give the lie to the canard that prejudice is always stronger than decency, that hate is more powerful than love. . . . You—rich and poor, Jew and Christian, black and white, professional and lay, men and women from every walk of life—you represent the true heart of a great city. You are Atlanta. You—and not the noisy rabble with their sheets and signs now slogging sullenly the sidewalks beyond these doors. Here is a truth we must resolve never to forget. Let none of us ever again fear to summon this truth so simply, so eloquently and so forcefully brought home to us tonight by our presence here.[4]

Later, when presenting an award to King, Rothschild declared that the minister "epitomize[d] the glowing hope of light restored to a world stumbling in the darkness of hate" and "symbolize[d] the challenge to all men that they become God's helpers to assure the dawn of a more radiant day."[5]

The King family was touched as never before. King's mother kept repeating, "To think this could happen in our lifetime! The grandson of a sharecropper!"[6] At the end of the evening, everyone stood and sang "We Shall Overcome." And the Kings were indeed overcome—with emotion and gratitude.

But despite the prestige of the Nobel Prize and despite the reassurance from Atlanta's top leaders that one of their native sons was on the right course, King's mission was still far from over. He now, somewhat reluctantly, set his sights on Selma, whose twenty-nine thousand people, more than half of whom were black, lived in an exact archetype of those towns in the Deep South that "expected niggers to know their place." Though the newly elected mayor, Joe Smitherman, and his director of police, "Hefty" Wilson Baker, wanted to avoid the violence and trauma that had occurred in other Southern cities when civil rights activists came to town, they were saddled with Sheriff Jim Clark, Coffee County's negrophobic rube-in-residence. With his gang of deputies, most of whom were Klan members, Clark made it his business to beat activists into submission. Until 1965, he succeeded.

James and Diane Bevel headed the SCLC office in Selma. After several unsuccessful efforts to get more blacks to register to vote, the local community pressed Bevel to involve King. In turn, Bevel convinced King that Selma would be the site of the movement's next big drama. As it was one of the most diehard, racially restrictive towns in the entire country, what would be more fitting than the birthplace of Bull Connor for a SCLC initiative?

King went to Selma for the first time in January 1965. When SNCC chairman (and future member of Congress) John Lewis pledged his organization's support for a campaign in Selma, King told Bevel and Hosea Williams to commence operations.

With the passage of the Civil Rights Act of 1964, segregation was no longer the major issue. The landmark legislation outlawed discrimination in hotels, motels, restaurants, and theaters, and it encouraged the integration of public schools by authorizing the attorney general to file suits to force desegregation. It also outlawed discrimination in employment in any business with more than twenty-five employees. But because the law did not address inequities in voter registration, that (plus easing the plight of blacks trapped in the decaying ghettoes of the North) became paramount for civil rights leaders.

For years, Southern blacks had been prevented from registering to vote. With farcical literacy demands and other chicanery, though time and again they presented themselves at the Selma courthouse to attempt to register, the results were always the same: None were approved. U.S. Deputy Attorney General Nicholas Katzenbach acknowledged: "The problem in the South of voting was primarily the problem of the literacy tests and the way in which they were administered. You had black Ph.D.'s who couldn't pass a literacy test and you had whites who could barely write their name who had no problems being registered to vote."[7]

Under SCLC directives, four hundred marchers descended on the town courthouse on January 18 to register to vote. While they normally would have been jailed for parading without a permit, Sheriff Clark was prevented by police director Baker from precipitating an incident. But King recognized his old nemesis, white supremacist J. B. Stoner, who was on hand, along with the chairman of the American Nazi Party chairman, George Lincoln Rockwell. Selma was certainly going to be an interesting affair. (Rockwell and his crew left two days later after Baker threatened to arrest them.)

Afterward, as King registered in the local King Albert hotel, the first black ever to do so, he was attacked by one of Stoner's followers. Baker arrested the attacker.

As the days went by and more and more people showed up to register to vote, Clark could no longer be held in check. Annoyed and frustrated, his anger at the boiling point, he went up and down the line of people who wanted to register, pushing and shoving them until he came to Annie Lee Cooper, who swirled around and slugged him. Clark staggered to his knees, and she hit him again. One deputy grabbed her from behind and tried to push her to the ground, but she stamped on his foot and jammed her elbow into his belly. Breaking loose, she turned to the sheriff, who was still trying to regain his balance, and she slugged him again. Clark and two deputies finally restrained her. She dared Clark to hit her and grabbed his club before he could get a decent swing at her. He finally wrenched the club free and brought it down on her head.

King, who was nearby, prevented enraged black men from stopping Clark. He feared what might happen if they attacked Clark, and he also wanted to be consistent with his policy of nonviolence. As long as newsmen were taking photos of the event, it was to the movement's advantage to let Clark continue with his attack, no matter how greatly it offended. Needless to say, the photographers had a field day.

After leaving to attend a dinner in his honor in Atlanta, King returned to Selma. His old "friend," Al Lingo, and his state troopers had also come to town at the request of the mayor.

By February 1, King was in jail along with more than two hundred fifty of his supporters. Later he would declare, "There are more Negroes in jail with me than there are on the voting rolls."[8] By then, hundreds of children and adults were already in Selma's prison.

While King was in jail, black militant Malcolm X visited Selma. King's aides in the SCLC were not pleased with the prospect of the former Nation of Islam spokesman addressing their troops, but some SNCC workers insisted that he be heard. When Malcolm finally got to the podium, he said that he didn't advocate violence but didn't favor nonviolence, either. "Whites," he warned, "better be glad that Martin Luther King is rallying the people because other forces are waiting to take over if he fails." Privately, Malcolm told Coretta Scott King that through his militancy he wanted to "give people an alternative to think about." Malcolm's stay in Selma was less then fleeting: three hours after he arrived, he drove off to the airport in Montgomery to attend a conference in London.[9]

(Later, reflecting on Malcolm after the Black Muslim was assassinated in early 1965, King sated that although Malcolm had said "some pretty passionate things against me," Malcolm had told Coretta that "he thought he could help me more by attacking me than praising me. He thought it would make it easier for me in the long run.")[10]

Issuing directives from his cell, King told Andrew Young to contact Jack Greenberg at the NAACP's Legal Defense Fund. Some legal remedy was needed for all the legal wranglings, injunctions, edicts, and what-not that were being issued against their actions in Selma.[11]

But the pressure of being in prison—and the depression that affected King whenever he was in jail—required that he quickly be released. The next day King posted bail, to the dismay of Harry Wachtel and others who wanted King's incarceration to turn into another Birmingham-jail scenario. Subsequently, King met with a congressional task force to discuss the situation in Selma. The task force returned to Washington, agreeing that some form of legislation was necessary to enforce federal statutes that already existed and that purportedly guaranteed blacks the right to vote.

In the meantime, King went to Montgomery, attempting to generate enthusiasm for a voter registration drive in that city. The next day he flew to Washington to meet with President Lyndon Johnson, Vice President Hubert Humphrey, and Attorney General Nicholas Katzenbach to discuss legislation that would eliminate the kind of activities prevalent in Selma.[12]

Upon returning to Selma, King learned that Clark and his henchmen had used cattle prods on a group of marching students. As enraged groups met to discuss a course of action, King advocated the further branching out of voter registration activities into more local communities. He then left for fund-raising talks in Michigan, and he attended to another issue that had been simmering on an altogether different flank: He called Clarence Jones, his main speechwriter, and asked him to draft several speeches decrying the growing animosity toward Jews that was becoming prevalent in SNCC and other militant black organizations.[13]

As King's voter registration campaign branched out into neighboring counties, Lingo's troopers were quick to put marchers to flight, shooting one, Jimmy Lee Jackson. While in his hospital bed, Jackson was charged with assaulting a police officer. On February 26, Jackson died. James Bevel delivered a sermon that night at Selma's Brown Chapel, expounding "on Esther 4:8, in which Mordecai warned Esther of an order to destroy the Jews, and charged her to go to the king and 'make request before him for her people.' ["I shall go to the king in spite of the law; and if I perish, I perish" (Esther 4:17).] He preached that the king now was Governor Wallace, who ran the state troopers and kept Negroes from voting. 'I must go see the king!' [Esther 4:16] he cried, and soon brought the whole church to its feet vowing to go on foot. . . . 'Be prepared to walk to Montgomery!' shouted Bevel."[14]

On March 3, King led the ceremonies in the church where Jimmy Lee Jackson had recently been elected deacon. He also approved Bevel's call for a fifty-mile march from Selma to Montgomery. On March 7, Bevel announced that King would march to the capital in Montgomery, the homeland of the Confederacy, to petition Governor Wallace to end "police brutality and grant Alabama Negroes the elective franchise." At the press conference, Bevel wore a yarmulke, something he'd been doing since his Freedom Riding days. He sometimes explained this affectation as an outgrowth of "his affection for the Hebrew prophets and other times as a protective device to keep himself out of jail, saying Mississippi sheriffs were so mystified by the sight of a Negro preacher in a 'Jewish beanie' they preferred to let him alone."[15]

From Washington, where he was meeting with President Johnson, King called his staff in Selma to tell them the march would have to be delayed for a day. Hosea Williams, however, would not wait. With five hundred marchers gathered that Sunday, Williams got permission from King to lead a march across the Pettus Bridge, the gateway to Montgomery. Together with John Lewis, Williams led the group directly toward a phalanx of state troopers, who had their clubs and tear gas ready. Moments later, the troopers charged the group. After that, Clark's men attacked with whips and with rubber tubing wrapped in barbed wire. Clark's hoodlums continued their attack even into the black section of town, going so far as to throw a black youth through the stained-glass window of a church. Some hundred forty people had to be hospitalized or treated for injuries.

On March 10, Morris Abram, then president of the American Jewish Committee, telegraphed President Johnson that the AJC

> shares your outrage at the shameful exhibition of brutality on the part of state and local police officers in preventing a march of Negro citizens in Selma, Alabama. All people of goodwill in America and around the world recoil at the use of tear gas, clubs, and whips direct-ed at Negroes demonstrating for the right to vote. We urge that you do all in your power to prevent the repetition of such events and to protect Negro citizens of Selma who have no other protections. We also applaud your directive to the Justice Department to intervene in the proceeding now pending in the Federal Court to enjoin Alabama officials from interfering with the right of Alabama citizens to demon-strate peaceably in support of the right to vote.[16]

The heads of other major Jewish organizations also railed at Washington to protest the Nazi-like tactics of Selma's police, includ-ing the National Community Relations Advisory Council, which was the coordinating agency for national and local Jewish organizations throughout the country.[17]

Disturbed that he was not in Selma to be with his people, King cabled several clergymen to come to Selma to bear witness. With film clips of the attack on the Selma marchers televised across the nation, the country was again repelled by Southern brutality, and King's telegrams brought over four hundred ministers, rabbis, nuns, priests, and lay personnel to Selma.

Plans were made for yet another attempt to reach Montgomery, and a petition was filed in federal court to enjoin Governor Wallace and Sheriff Clark from using force to stop the march. Judge Frank Johnson issued a restraining order against all parties. Despite this pro-hibition, the entreaties of Attorney General Nicholas Katzenbach, and representatives of President Johnson himself, King gathered about fifteen hundred marchers to cross from Selma into Montgomery.

When they reached the Pettus Bridge, they were confronted by the state police. As the injunction was read to them the clerics prayed, and as if in answer to their prayer, the troopers disbanded. Yet, instead of proceeding forward, King ordered the marchers to return to Selma. Unknown to them, the encounter had been orchestrated.

Leroy Collins, the head of the Federal Community Relations Service, had "worked out an understanding with . . . [King] that he would cross the bridge and face law enforcement officers, but not attempt to continue to Montgomery. Collins had even given . . . [King] a hand-drawn map depicting the march route . . . [King] later said that he knew it would have been impossible to break through the troopers' lines."[18]

But the deal had its aftereffects, especially among members of SNCC. The SNCC contingent had anticipated violence; they had come, in fact, to have their heads bloodied. When they were denied their carnage, they denounced King and left. A few, like John Lewis, stayed. King was distressed by this break in the ranks, but he would soon be further distressed by the death of the Rev. James Reeb, a white Unitarian minister from Detroit.

Reeb was one of the clerics who had answered King's call. When he and a group of ministers were set upon by white toughs, Reeb was slammed in the head by a baseball bat and soon died. Protests about Reeb's death came from around the country, and Rabbi Eugene Lipman of Temple Sinai in Washington flew to Selma to represent the Commission on Social Action of the Reform Movement's Union of American Hebrew Congregations at the memorial services for Reeb.

Though King was grateful for the support, the irony that the death of Jimmy Lee Jackson had not produced a similar response was not lost on him. President Johnson subsequently appeared on television to announce that he was sending a civil rights voting bill to Congress. "What happened in Selma," he said, "is part of the larger movement which reaches into every section and state of America. It is the effort of American Negroes to secure for themselves the full blessing of American life. Their cause must be our cause, too. Because . . . all of us . . . must overcome the crippling legacy of bigotry and injustice." In conclusion, Johnson invoked the anthem of the civil rights movement: "And we shall overcome."[19]

With the anti-march order lifted, and Judge Johnson issuing an injunction against Clark and Governor Wallace, some thirty-two hundred marchers gathered to travel to Montgomery on March 21. Among them was Don G. Lebby, who wrote before he left Cleveland:

> Tomorrow's promises are not enough. It did not help the Christians facing death in Rome to know that tomorrow all would be changed. The tortured prisoners of the Inquisition were not aided by any promise of a free future. Much closer to my heart is this aching thought. How could it help the prisoner if the Nazi guard said, "Don't worry—tomorrow will be a brighter day," as he turned on the gas.
>
> It is not enough to sit quietly and agree. Cain was wrong. He was his brother's keeper. Every man has an obligation to every other man. I can not be satisfied to sit comfortably in committee rooms and chambers. There has to come a time in my life to prove to myself that I am what I profess to be. I must be counted and I must be visible. My wife shares my convictions.
>
> We leave tonight for Alabama. And we are afraid.[20]

Surrounded by Alabama National Guardsmen, who had been federalized, and by U.S. Marshals and military police, King finally had the protection he had so longed for. As Rabbi Friedlander, a participant in the March, would later record:

> Some images stand out in my mind: Professor Abraham Heschel marching in front of me, firm and erect, the wind catching his white beard and hair. . . . A Negro lady (Mrs. Foster), walking next to me, pointed out the exact spot on that highway where Alabama troop-

ers had beaten her to the ground. "Going all the way this time," she smiled, and waved to some friends along the road. . . .

But the heart of the march was the group of Negro marchers from Alabama who wanted the vote, each with a red band on his arm, still in mourning for Jimmy Lee Jackson and their other, unknown, martyrs. It was *their* march; and perhaps our main reason for being with them was the fact that our white skins gave them some protection from the rifles ready in the swampland surrounding us. . . .

If nothing else, we had finally felt the living essence of the words of Amos: "Are ye not as the children of the Ethiopians unto Me, O children of Israel?"[21]

As the march progressed, skullcaps became a symbol of the movement. James Bevel, as mentioned before, had worn one for several years, but now the marchers called for "freedom caps" of their own. The demand for yarmulkes was so great that an order was wired for delivery of a thousand caps when the marchers would arrive in Montgomery and demonstrate at the state capitol. When the group finally reached Montgomery days later, having surged to some twenty-five thousand people, the event was heralded as the greatest day ever for the civil rights.

On March 25, as the throng gathered at the steps of the state capitol in Montgomery, Rabbi Maurice Eisendrath, president of the Reform Movement's Union of American Hebrew Congregations, was asked by King to address the crowd.[22]

But the battleground would claim another victim before it was all over. Viola Liuzzo, a white woman from Detroit, had driven to Selma to offer her help in the battle for equal rights. She was shot by Klansmen during a high-speed chase on an Alabama highway.

Days later, when George Wallace finally met with a biracial committee to discuss black claims, ten coffins were placed on the sidewalk outside the capitol—one for each of the civil rights workers killed in Alabama.[23]

Summing up the events of Selma, the American Jewish Committee's *Newsletter* declared:

> The peaceful Civil Rights March on Washington in 1963 was a Sunday picnic compared to this spring's brutal trek from Selma to Montgomery. . . . Though violence, social protest and power struggles are no strangers to this country . . . Selma's agony intensified public involvement in a way that has rarely happened before in American history. . . . [T]his time, the public—certainly large sections of it—was far from neutral. Nor has the Church, Protestant and Catholic, ever made such a massive and highly visible commitment to overt social action as it has in the struggle for the Negroes' right to vote.
>
> For Judaism, . . . the race crisis represents a moral challenge, since Judaism has contributed to the concepts behind the Negro struggle by its historic insistence on the rights and dignity of the individual. It is generally acknowledged that Jews have been among the leaders in advancing legislation and supporting court action to expand and enforce equality of opportunity for Negroes. Many Jews, including rabbis, certainly greater in number than their proportion in the population, have joined the struggle as individuals. Despite this, the net impression remains that organized Jewry does not appear sufficiently visible as the tide of social protest flows into the streets and the marketplace.
>
> Many factors inhibit full participation by Jews. Broadening currents of anti-Semitism among Negroes, explosive confrontations with Negroes in urban settings—schools, business, neighborhoods—surely contribute their share to increasing the ambivalence of some Jews towards active engagement in overt social protest.
>
> Yet, from their own experience, Jews are bound to recognize that no matter how comfortable the status quo may appear to be . . . , it will not last long in a sick society. The quest for Negro equality, if it is to be won without total revolution, cannot be allowed to become a conflict between black and white. Jews know too that rights can only be achieved and reinforced with allies in the society who recognize the true validity of the cause as a problems for all Americans.

Finally, Jews know that their rights are intimately linked with the rights of others, that prejudice is contagious and indivisible . . . , that those who are anti-Negro today may well turn out to be anti-Jewish tomorrow. . . . In taking full and effective action to advance the Negro pursuit of equality, Jews are acting in the interest of balance and stability among peers rather than accommodation of "inferiors." The realistic demands of the social revolution going on throughout the country requires of Jews that they strive to overcome the agony of indecision.[24]

A few months later, in August, President Johnson signed the Voting Rights Act of 1965. King would view the Selma to Montgomery march as a vindication of his beliefs:

I saw Protestants, Catholics and Jews standing, singing and praying together. I saw them marching together from Selma to Montgomery. So, I can say that the church, the synagogues are giving support to the movement now in a way that we haven't known it before. . . . I am absolutely convinced . . . that when we in the religious institutions of our nation really decide to stand firm on this issue, we will achieve not merely a desegregated society, but an integrated society which we all seek.[25]

16

Afrocentrists' New Target: Israel

O n May 15, 1948, Jews in Palestine announced the creation of the modern State of Israel. Immediately, Jews, many of them survivors of the Holocaust, were fighting the Goliath-sized Arab armies that poured into Israel from all sides. A "conscience-stricken" world watched, especially because the British, who had administered Palestine, had let Arabs arm themselves while forbidding Jews to do the same. But the Jews won a cease-fire the next year and settled into a wary, often violent relationship with their Arab and Palestinian neighbors.

The great black intellectual and writer W. E. B. Du Bois depicted Zionism as being conveyed by "young and forward thinking Jews bringing a new civilization into an old land and building up that land out of the ignorance, disease and poverty into which it had fallen, and by democratic methods to build a new and peculiarly fateful modern state."[1]

Church-going, Bible-reading African Americans have a great and long-standing affection for the Holy Land of the Bible. Their churches in the North and the South, from earliest times, have carried names like Mt. Carmel, Mt. Hebron, Mt. Canaan, and Gilboa— all sites in Israel. And names like Galilee, Jerusalem, Nazareth, Jericho, Jordan, Bethlehem, the Mount of Olives, Gethsemane, Mount Zion have long been familiar ones in spirituals, Sunday sermons, and black religious worship.[2] Martin Luther King, Jr. was born into this social milieu—even his father had made a pilgrimage to the Holy Land.[3] In college, he studied the philosophy of theologian Reinhold Niebuhr, who "insisted on the right of Jews to live anywhere in the world they chose but at the same time to have the right to express their unique heritage with a national homeland."[4]

Among black Christians, approval of Jewish rights to the Holy Land would be echoed time and again. On his return from a visit to Israel, Therion E. Cobbs, the editor-in-chief of *Religious Literature of the African Methodist Episcopal Church*, declared:

> The cry of Israel is a clear clarion call to American and European Jews . . . alike who possess a common cultural-religious background. The cry of Israel was voiced by Emma Lazarus and was inscribed on the Statue of Liberty in the harbour of New York: "Give me your tired, your hungry, your bleeding [sic] masses yearning to be free. . . ."
>
> And in the inevitable agony of the war-ravaged peoples of Europe, Asia and Africa, for months and even years ahead, there can be no miserly calculating about the things which we as fellow human beings are called upon to deliver to those who have suffered the ravages of war, prejudice and discrimination. More than our existence depends upon the answer which we give. It affects our very right to exist.[5]

The people of Israel held a special place in King's thinking. During Israel's 1956 war with Egypt, he wrote: "There is something in the very nature of the universe which is on the side of Israel in its struggle with every Egypt."[6]

King visited Gandhi's India in February 1959, then returned to Montgomery by a circuitous route that took him through Jordan, Egypt, and Greece. In March, King visited Jerusalem and Jericho, then still in Arab hands. Though Jordan refused to let him into the Jewish quarter in the Old City of Jerusalem, King often spoke of the adventure and excitement of being in the Holy City and the Holy Land. In fact, the last speech he gave before his death specifically referred to his trip on the Jericho road.

In 1964, after receiving his Nobel Prize, King entertained the idea of visiting Israel, especially after receiving a formal invitation from Israel's largest labor union, the Histadrut. But pressing U.S. domestic issues prevented him from making the journey. What was left unsaid in his response to the Histadrut was the likelihood that traveling to Israel might have caused him grave problems. As growing black nationalism made alliance with brown-skinned Arabs more acceptable than a relationship with white Israelis, King surely did not want to give ammunition to those anti-Israel propagandists who were beginning to dominate certain segments of the black community. Long supported by Jews, and long recognizing the importance of a Jewish State, especially after the Holocaust, King was no doubt counseled by his advisors not to engage in any confrontation that would further alienate him from the more radical elements of Afro-Americanism. The new anti-Zionist rumblings—usually were fueled by outright anti-Semitism—that were trying to drive a wedge between blacks and Jews were already having economic repercussions: Jewish contributions to civil rights activities were drying up because of the virulent new African American polemic, and advocating any Jewish cause would surely adversely affect King and the SCLC in parts of his own community.

But in the latter part of 1966, in consultation with Harlem's Rev. Sandy Ray, King concocted a plan that he hoped would spark a peace movement between Israel and its neighbors. In November, he sent Andrew Young to Israel to plan a program in the Holy Land. Young flew to Tel Aviv, where he wanted to make arrangements for a pilgrimage of five thousand people. But Israel didn't have sufficient hotel space to accommodate a tour of this size, so Young drove to Jordan to make arrangements there as well. He began negotiating with both sides for the Mandelbaum Gate, a highly restricted entry point between the Jordanian and Israeli parts of Jerusalem to be opened for his group. Officials in the Israeli and Jordanian tourism offices were "highly receptive" to Young's plans, and both Israel and Jordan agreed to cooperate to build an amphitheater on the Sea of Galilee, where Martin would preach from the water. This tour would bring a great deal of money to both countries, so they had good reason to be agreeable.

King had calculated that the broad, long-term economics of the Middle East would require Jews and Arabs to work together. So if this pilgrimage could demonstrate the potential of tourism, and especially religious-based tourism, to heal some of the wounds between Arab and Jew, then, as Young later reflected, "Martin Luther King could have changed the history of the region by demonstrating how much every one had to gain by working together."[7]

But it was not to be. Egyptian jets were shot down over Gaza as the 1967 Six Day War broke out on the day that Young left Tel Aviv after yet another round of negotiating to make the pilgrimage a reality.

Just before the start of the war, King, Reinhold Niebuhr, and Bishop Stephen Gill Spotswood of Washington signed an open letter to President Johnson in the *New York Times* calling for the United States to honor its commitments to Israel.[8] Once the ad was published, King was concerned that he had made a political blunder.

According to Murray Friedman's *What Went Wrong: The Creation and Collapse of the Black-Jewish Alliance:*

> In a conversation with Levison and his other New York advisers the . . . [day after the ad appeared], King admitted to being confused. He had never actually seen the ad before it appeared, he told them. When he did, he was not happy with it. He felt it was unbalanced and pro-Israel, although he observed that it would probably help him with the Jewish community.
>
> After carefully weighing the situation, his advisers, even the Jewish ones, suggested in effect that King carry water on both shoulders. Since war settles nothing, as Levison put it, King could adopt a peace position without taking sides. While agreeing that the territorial integrity of Israel and its right to a homeland were incontestable, King should urge that all other questions be settled by negotiation. Such a position, said Levison, would serve to keep the Arab friendship and the Israeli friendship. King agreed.
>
> Two days later, in a conference call with . . . [several advisors, including Levinson and Andrew Young], just prior to a speech on Vietnam, King again asked for their views. SNCC and others in the black community had attacked him for signing the advertisement. . . . He was in a real dilemma, he said. . . . A news article in the *Times* had described the ad as a "total endorsement" of Israel, King said.
>
> His advisers suggested that he simply back the UN call for a cease-fire. King did not have to worry too much about losing the support of the Jewish community . . . [they said], so long as he strode very lightly and stressed an end to violence.[9]

When the war actually broke out, however, King was reticent about commenting on it. Though his Jewish allies expected him to support Israel, King remained silent on the issue. Jewish organizations that had long supported King noticed his silence. An internal memo of the American Jewish Committee noted:

> Martin Luther King spoke twice in Washington last week [in early June, 1967]. On both occasions . . . he failed to make any statement about the war in the Middle East. His first speech was billed as a discussion of international problems, however the war having broken out probably caught King flatfooted, because he did not discuss any international matter that night. Rather, he gave a lengthy review of the history of the struggle for domestic civil rights, which was not particularly impressive. He spoke again for the Capitol Press Club at its major annual dinner here on Saturday, June 10th. The Capitol Press Club is the association of negro [sic] journalists in Washington. . . . While King did discuss Vietnam and maintain his position, again he made no reference to the war in the Middle East other than to acknowledge that it did exist, and to state that time did not permit discussing it. . . . The fact that King twice in the week failed to discuss the war has a variety of implications, which I think the recipients of this memo can infer on their own.[10]

The aftereffects of the war brought about a strange dichotomy in the black psyche. Before the war, most blacks had viewed the birth and success of Israel as a powerful, compelling vision from which they could borrow for their own campaign for freedom. According to an article published in the American Jewish Committee's magazine:

> Far stronger than Negro resentment against Jews is Negro identification with the Jewish people: not only with the Jew as victim, but with the Jew as triumphant battler against the corrosion of victimization from the sermons and spirituals of the anti-bellum Negro church, which spoke and sang of a people marching out of slavery in Egypt and shattering the walls of Jericho, to the contemporary images of the fighting Israeli and the heroes of the Warsaw ghetto.
>
> Indeed the emergence of the new State of Israel, according to the testimony of Negro leaders, had much to do with the affirmation of Negro selfhood both in the new African nationalisms and in the Negro revolt here at home.[11]

After Israel's extraordinary victory in the war, radical black organizations seized upon Israel's success as evidence of a racial and religious war upon the "brown men" of the Middle East. Rabbi Richard Rubenstein wrote a few months after the war:

Since the Arab-Israeli Six Day War, the Jewish community has witnessed a rapid multiplication of its enemies, especially on the left. The same circumstances which led Negro intellectuals to see themselves as victims of internal colonialism have also led them to identify with the Arab cause. They regard the Israelis as technologically competent European settlers who bear the same relationship to the Arabs as did European settlers to natives elsewhere in the world. They view Arab attempts to exterminate Israel as a legitimate employment of violence by the oppressed against those who have established themselves in the midst of Arab territory by imperialist penetration. It matters little whether this picture is distorted. It is the image an increasing number of influential Negroes have of Israel.[12]

As growing ant-Semitism among blacks found voice in anti-Zionist harangues, King finally made his position clear in an article that appeared in the *Saturday Review* two months after the war ended:

Zionism is nothing less than the dream and ideal of the Jewish people returning to live in their own land. The Jewish people, the Scriptures tell us, once enjoyed a flourishing Commonwealth in the Holy Land. From this they were expelled by the Roman tyrant, the same Romans who cruelly murdered Our Lord. Driven from their homeland, their nation in ashes, forced to wander the globe, the Jewish people time and again suffered the lash of whichever tyrant happened to rule over them.

The Negro people ... know what it is to suffer the torment of tyranny under rulers not of our choosing. Our brothers in Africa have begged, pleaded, requested—DEMANDED the recognition and realization of our inborn right to live in peace under our own sovereignty in our own country.

> How easy it should be, for anyone who holds dear this inalien-
> able right of all mankind, to understand and support the right of the
> Jewish People to live in their ancient Land of Israel. All men of good
> will exult in the fulfillment of God's promise, that his People should
> return in joy to rebuild their plundered land.[13]

But still, Israel's victory posed many political problems for King. Murray Friedman wrote, King "had always admired Israel; he saw it as the source of the Judeo-Christian tradition embraced by most blacks. Indeed, he had urged blacks to learn from and promote a pragmatic version of Zionism. . . . [But] as a pacifist, he felt it necessary to oppose killing, whether it occurred in Vietnam or the Middle East. Moreover, he had to concern himself . . . with the pro-Arab views of black nationalists and separatists. They already distrusted him, and his endorsement of Israel's preemptive attack on Egypt would make matters worse."[14]

The situation worsened when King began to contemplate leading the interracial pilgrimage to the Holy Land on which Young had been working. King wondered whether the trip, coming so soon after the war, made sense, since Arabs, and probably African and Asian countries, too, would interpret the trip as endorsing Israel's military actions. He was especially worried that for most of his stay he would be in Jerusalem, which Israel had already annexed "and any way you say it, they don't plan to give it back." Young encouraged King to develop strong views on the Middle East, partly by cultivating personal contacts with Arabs because their position had had scant exposure in this country. While saying that Israel had been in danger of extinction, Levinson seemed to be more troubled by the role of the "Zionist Jew" in the Middle East, and he wondered what ghetto blacks would think of King if he took a group of middle-class blacks and whites to the Holy Land under the present circumstances.[15]

In the midst of all this, anti-Israel diatribes increased among blacks. Soon after convening in Chicago in September 1967 to explore the possibility of a third-party ticket in the 1968 Presidential election, the National Conference of New Politics was divided along racial lines. The conference of mostly left-leaning civil rights, anti-poverty, and peace activists was confronted with blacks demanding that they have a majority voting bloc on any decision making, regardless of their actual numbers. The assembly, loath to challenge the blacks, genuflected to them and labeled Israel an imperialist state.

Many in the more establishment black community broke from the resolutions of the convention. Samuel Jackson, the highest ranking black in the Johnson administration, wrote to the Anti-Defamation League that "the views expressed in that resolution are not those held by the great majority of blacks in this country. We are both aware and appreciative of the role which Israel has played in the economic development of many of the African nations."[16]

The Jewish community was in an uproar, and an open letter from the heads of major Jewish American organizations—many of whom had supported civil rights and the SCLC for years—went to King asking about not just the SCLC's participation in the convention, but about his own in the entire notion of these "new" politics:

Our organizations share a deep commitment to full equality in an integrated, plural society. We believe that its attainment demands action by a coalition of groups for accelerated and dramatic social change. We have admired and respected your advocacy of these goals and your leadership over the years.

Now we are profoundly distressed by the recent New Politics Conventions. The apartheid of the adopted structure and the lack of democratic procedure; the absence of any specific constructive program for the advancement of equal opportunity; the anti-Semitism in spite of disavowals; the irrational anti-Israel resolution; all are disturbing and destructive. We believe that they also are antithetical to everything you have stood for.

Because of . . . your name on the National Council of the Conference for New Politics, we fear that these destructive positions may gain a show of respectability. We urge you to disassociate yourself publicly from the malevolence which found expression in the resolutions of the New Politics Convention.[17]

King responded to his old friend Morris Abram that had he been present, "I would have made it crystal clear that I could not have supported any resolution calling for . . . a condemnation of Israel."[18]

In the face of continued Jewish concern, the SCLC's newsletter declared: "SCLC and Dr. King have repeatedly stated that the Middle East problem embodies the related questions of security and development. Israel's right to exist as a state in security is incontestable."[19]

Although King was becoming increasingly amenable to certain more radical views, such as those expressed in his critique of capitalism and of America's military presence in Vietnam, he never endorsed anti-Semitism or anti-Israel feeling, both of which were gaining greater currency in left-wing circles. He was still sure that an alliance between blacks and Jews was fundamental to civil rights progress. The resolution adopted in Chicago and SNCC's new direction therefore reflected a major difference between SCLC and SNCC and a dramatic split between the older, more established leaders and the younger blacks who were unwilling to submerge ideological differences to coalition politics. Soon, even moderate blacks were forced into silence or went along with the trend. Indeed, King was the last major black leader to promote the legitimacy of Zionism within the black community.[20] At the convention of the Rabbinical Assembly in March 1968, for instance, nine months after the Six Day War, King declared:

On the Middle East crisis, we have had various responses. The response of some of the so-called young militants again does not represent the position of the vast majority of Negroes. There are some who are color-consumed and they see a kind of mystique in being colored, and anything non-colored is condemned. . . . I think it is necessary to say that what is basic and what is needed in the Middle East is peace. Peace for Israel is one thing. Peace for the Arab side of that world is another thing. Peace for Israel means security, and we must stand with all of our might to protect its right to exist, its territorial integrity. I see Israel, and never mind saying it, as one of the great outposts of democracy in the world and a marvelous example of what can be done, how desert land almost can be transformed into an oasis of brotherhood and democracy. Peace for Israel means security and that security must be a reality.[21]

Those comments were perhaps the strongest that King had ever uttered about Israel. Perhaps he was evincing a growing trend among Christian theologians about the place of Israel in the world. As A. Roy Eckhardt, a Lehigh University professor of religious studies and a Methodist minister, wrote:

Israel is the one place that enables Christians to be redeemed from the temptations which habitually afflict them as a majority in the presence of Jews. Here is a land where Jews can be what they *are*, free from the sufferance of everyone, a place where the Christian duality of "human" and "religious" is told to hold its tongue and keep its distance. It is a good thing for the Christian soul to be forced to live without power, especially power over Jews. Perhaps Israel—yes, a *secular* Israel—can help a little to teach the church the meaning of trust in God.[22]

In what would be his final speech, King, in Memphis on April 3, 1968, recalled his own trip to the Holy Land nine years before. He especially remembered traveling on the legendary road from Jerusalem to Jericho, referred to in the parable of the Good Samaritan (Luke 10, 29-37):

One day a man came to Jesus; and he wanted to raise some questions about some vital matters in life. . . . Jesus immediately pulled that question from mid-air, and placed it on a dangerous curve between Jerusalem and Jericho. And he talked about a certain man, who fell among thieves. You remember that a Levite and a priest passed by on the other side. They didn't stop to help him. And finally a man of another race came by. He got down from his beast, . . . administered first aid, and helped the man in need. Jesus . . . [said that] this was the good man, . . . the great man, because he had the capacity to project the "I" into the "thou," and to be concerned about his brother.

Now you know, . . . I'm going to tell you what my imagination tells me [about why the priest and the Levite didn't stop]. It's possible that these men were afraid. You see, the Jericho road is a dangerous road. I remember when Mrs. King and I were first in Jerusalem. We rented a car and drove from Jerusalem down to Jericho. And as soon as we got on that road, I said to my wife, "I can see why Jesus used this as a setting for his parable." It's a winding, meandering road. It's really conducive for ambushing. You start out in Jerusalem, which is about . . . 1,200 feet above sea level. And by the time you get down to Jericho . . . , you're about 2,200 feet below sea level. That's a dangerous road. In the days of Jesus, it came to be known as the "Bloody Pass." And you know, it's possible that the priest and the Levite looked over that man on the ground and wondered if the robbers were still around. Or it's possible that they felt that the man on the ground was merely faking. And he was acting like he had been robbed and hurt, in order to . . . lure them there for quick and easy seizure. And so the first question that the Levite asked was, "If I stop to help this man, what will happen to me?" But then the Good Samaritan came by. And he reversed the question: "If I do not stop to help this man, what will happen to him?"[23]

Hours after he gave this speech, King was dead—a victim of the fear and hate he had fought to dispel, a traveler on his own road, one that had proved to be even more dangerous for King than the Jericho road had been for that Biblical stranger long ago.

17

Friendship Lost

Throughout his adult life, Martin Luther King, Jr., had Jewish friends: political advisers Stanley Levison and Harry Wachtel; literary agent Joan Daves; rabbis Abraham Joshua Heschel, Maurice Eisendrath, and Israel Dresner; attorneys William Kunstler, Jack Greenberg, and Morris Abram. King was always true to the credo he articulated in the *SCLC Newsletter* in July, 1964: "I solemnly pledge to do my utmost to uphold the fair name of the Jews. Not only because we need their friendship, and surely we do, but mainly because bigotry in any form is an affront to us all."[1]

And despite the growing antipathy between blacks and Jews, especially as SNCC and other black organizations became more radical, he always maintained an allegiance to Jews and refused to indulge in another side of the same hatred that had targeted blacks for so long:

Modern psychology has a word that is used probably more than any other word in modern psychology; it is the word maladjusted. . . . [T]here are certain things in our world and our nation of which I am proud to be maladjusted and to which I call upon you to be maladjusted, and all men of good will to be maladjusted, until the good societies realize I never intend to adjust myself to segregation and racial discrimination. I never intend to become adjusted to religious bigotry.[2]

Through all this, King continually met with Jewish leaders and spoke out against black anti-Semitism:

How could there be anti-Semitism among Negroes when our Jewish friends have demonstrated their commitment to the principle of tolerance and brotherhood not only in the form of sizable contributions, but in many other tangible ways, and often at great personal sacrifice? Can we ever express our appreciation to the rabbis who chose to give moral witness with us in St. Augustine . . . ? Need I remind anyone of the awful beating suffered by Rabbi Arthur Lelyveld of Cleveland when he joined the civil rights workers ... in Hattiesburg, Mississippi? And who can ever forget the sacrifice of two Jewish lives, Andrew Goodman and Michael Schwerner, in the swamps of Mississippi? It would be impossible to record the contribution that the Jewish people have made toward the Negro's struggle for freedom— it has been so great.[3]

Just a few years earlier, Louis Martin, an influential columnist with a black newspaper, the *Chicago Defender*, had said much the same thing: "No other minority in American life, including ourselves, has fought more vigorously or more effectively against prejudice than the Jews."[4]

Nevertheless, by the mid-1960s, a new dynamic between blacks and Jews had begun to assert itself, especially among Northern blacks. A 1964 poll determined that 47 percent of blacks subscribed to anti-

Semitic beliefs versus 35 percent of whites. Another study, this one of blacks who had migrated from the South to the North, found that they harbored "an amazingly high percentage of anti-Semitism, reflecting some of the white attitudes of that region."[5] Anti-Semitism found root among blacks because its virus had contaminated them while they or their relatives or friends were in the South. Moreover, their anger festered because they were in the poverty, inadequate ghetto housing, and job discrimination of the North—which had largely been untouched by the civil rights movement. A young black civil rights leader in Philadelphia damned every Jew participating in the civil rights movement as "a goddamn phoney"; Malcolm X said the six million Jews who had perished in the Holocaust had "brought it on themselves"; an African American in Philadelphia somewhat torturously reasoned that "all those Jews in the civil rights marches and going down South—you know why they do it? They do it to take the heat off of themselves. They've got a bad conscience because they live on black dollars."[6]

Blacks saw Jews prospering and living in fine suburban homes or uptown apartments while they themselves suffered in poverty amid roaches and drugs and crime: Their "rights" had improved, but the quality of their life had remained static. As Harvard sociologist Nathan Glazer wrote at the time, even after key Supreme Court decisions favorable to them and after landmark civil rights legislation, blacks were furious "that the system of formal equality produces so little for them." Glazer was especially concerned that the same frictions that had long been common between lower-class blacks and Jews were now percolating among some black leaders and the new black middle class. He anticipated a rather ominous outcome for what had been a rather unique relationship between blacks and Jews.[7]

As Levison told the American Jewish Congress while trying to explain this phenomenon:

In this mood of resentment, hostility and disenchantment, the Jew is a special target. He is both the liberal white and the traditional scapegoat. Anti-Semitism among Negroes thus becomes both an outlet for anti-white feelings and a method whereby the Negro asserts his identity with Christian America. The Jews are alien "by birth and religion; he is Christian and a native American. He thus is able to find a way of solidarizing and identifying himself with the dominant white group."

In most cases, moreover, the contact that the average Negro has with the Jew is the kind that, by its very nature, produces hostility. It is an "exploitative relationship—one of landlord and tenant, employer and employee, small shopkeeper and customer." In a city such as New York more Negroes work for Jews than for any other white group; more Negroes buy from Jewish storekeepers; and more Negroes have Jewish landlords. In all of these relationships the Jew appears as the exploiter, gouger, abuser—whether in fact or stereotyped.

Add to this the rise of a new Negro middle class that brings the Negro into daily competition with Jewish business and professional men; the increasing Negro nationalism that is expressed by closer identification with the colored peoples of Africa (and the hostility to Israel which this inspires), and the rising political power of Negroes in areas where Jewish politicians have formally held sway—and you have some idea of the many areas of conflict that are responsible for the increasing anti-Semitism which is occurring today.[8]

Of the leading civil rights groups, SNCC perhaps suffered the greatest change. It had started as a younger, Ghandian extension of King's SCLC, led and manned mostly by middle-class, very religious blacks in their early and mid-20s. But starting around 1962 and especially after 1964, the leaders of SNCC began to see nonviolence as nothing more than a tactic, especially after riots in Philadelphia, Harlem, and Watts convinced them they could channel the discontent in these ghettoes to their revolutionary advantage. A trip to Africa in 1964 sealed SNCC's fate. Impressed with Africans' struggle for independence from colonialism, SNCC leaders returned to the United States with a reinvigorated militancy. Bob Moses, SNCC's chairman, told a Berkeley audience that he was there as a member of the Third World. He refused the assistance of the NAACP's battalions of lawyers, which he deemed too moderate. Similarly, Stokely Carmichael, who became chairman in 1966 when Moses was deemed too temperate, presided over the expulsion of whites from the organization. His cry of "Black Power" ushered in a new era in African-American politics.[9]

Even though Roy Innis, head of the Congress of Racial Equality (CORE), warned that "a black man would be crazy to publicly repudiate anti-Semitism," King tried to reason with what he saw as the young hotheads who were promulgating the new mood:

> Jews have power, but if you ever accuse them of power, they deny it. Catholics have power, but they always deny it. In a pluralistic society, to have real power you have to deny it. And if you go around claiming power, the whole society turns on you and crushes you. . . . If you really have power, you don't need a slogan.[10]

As Jew's fear of black anti-Semitism increased and Jewish commitment to civil rights wavered, King tried to convince Jews that "the anti-Semitism we find in the black community is almost completely an urban Northern ghetto phenomenon, virtually nonexistent in the South. This is because the Negro in the ghetto confronts the Jew in two dissimilar roles. He confronts the Jew in the role of being his most consistent and trusted ally in his struggle for justice in the civil rights movement. Probably more than any other ethnic group, the Jew has been sympathetic and has stood as an ally." It was Jews' other "role" that was fueling some blacks' contempt for Jews, a role that cast them as exploiter and manipulator. King explained, "The Negro confronts the Jew in the ghetto as the owner of the store around the corner where he pays more for less. But the fact is that the Jewish landlord or shopkeeper is not operating on the basis of Jewish ethics; he is operating on the basis of a marginal businessman. It is just simply that, and consequently the conflicts come into being." King's prescription for the new black-Jewish tensions was the same one he had been offering for more than a decade as the solution to tensions between blacks and whites: "The answer to this is for all people to condemn injustice wherever it exists."[11]

Yet, even in the South, where King claimed there was minimal anti-Semitism, anti-Jewish feelings began rise. King attributed this in part to "disappointment." Blacks, he said, had hoped that Jews, "a minority group, with a history of vilification and persecution that indeed was longer and as bitter as . . . [theirs], would be more sympathetic to . . . [their] plight. Although many Southern Negroes appreciate the exposed position of Southern Jews, many had nevertheless expected that Jews would have spoken out more forcefully than they had against exploitation and oppression."[12]

Despite King's efforts to retain his Jewish allies, anti-Jewish feelings began to surface even within the SCLC itself. Hosea Williams was charged with making anti-Semitic statements in remarks at Spelman College in Atlanta when he said that "the Jews did not vote since 'they were too busy making money in their stores.'"[13]

As black-Jewish tensions worsened, American Jewish Congress head Will Maslow resigned in 1966 from a biracial committee after he was subjected to an anti-Jewish diatribe, and King wrote in New York's *Amsterdam News* that he was "saddened" that Clifford Brown, a CORE official, had shouted during a heated school desegregation meeting in Mount Vernon, New York, that Hitler had not killed enough Jews. "Actually," he stated,

I do not view this horrible outburst as anti-Jewish. I see it as anti-man and anti-God. It would be a statement to harshly condemn coming from anyone. It is singularly despicable coming from the lips of a black man.

For black people, who have been tortuously burned in the crucible of hatred for centuries, should have become so purified of hate in those scorching flames as to be instinctively intolerant of intolerance. In the struggle for human rights, as well as in the struggle for the upward march of our civilization, we have deep need for the partnership, fellowship and courage of our Jewish Brother.[14]

Despite all this, many Jews' commitment to black causes did not waiver. As journalist Charles Silberman wrote in the American Jewish Congress' magazine in 1966, "anti-Semitism is irrelevant to a consideration of Jewish responsibility because, in the most fundamental sense, that responsibility stems from *us* and not from Negroes. . . . What we do . . . —what we are *obliged* to do—we are obliged to do . . . not because of what Negroes do or don't do, not because of what Negroes are or are not—but because of what we are ourselves, because of our obligation, in the prophetic injunction, to do justice."[15]

Yet, the plague of anti-Semitism worsened and increased. SNCC's new alignment with the Third World, especially the Arab world intensified its gleeful criticism of Israel after the 1967 Six Day War. A cartoon in the *SNCC Newsletter* showed the Israeli general Moshe Dayan with dollar signs on his epaulets; another depicted boxer Muhammad Ali with a noose around his neck while he was supported by a hand decorated with the Star of David and a dollar sign. Meanwhile, a Black Panther magazine published this doggerel:

We're gonna burn their towns and that ain't all,
We're gonna piss upon the Wailing Wall.
And then we'll get Kosygin and DeGaulle.
That will be ecstasy, killing every Jew we see.[16]

To hide their overt anti-Semitism, black radicals adopted a platform condemning Zionism. King quickly unmasked this charade:

You declare, my friend, that you do not hate the Jews, you are merely "anti-Zionist." And I say, let the truth ring forth from the high mountain tops, let it echo through the valleys of God's green earth: When people criticize Zionism, they mean Jews—this is God's own truth. Anti-Semitism . . . has been and remains a blot on the soul of mankind. In this we are in full agreement. So know also this: anti-Zionist is inherently anti-Semitic, and ever will be so. . . .

The anti-Semite rejoices at any opportunity to vent his malice. The times have made it unpopular, in the West, to proclaim openly a hatred of the Jews. This being the case, the anti-Semite must constantly seek new forms and forums for his poison. How he must revel in the new masquerade! He does not hate the Jews, he is just "anti-Zionist"!

My friend, I do not accuse you of deliberate anti-Semitism . . . But I know you have been misled—as others have been—into thinking you can be "anti-Zionist" and yet remain true to these heartfelt principles that you and I share. Let my words echo in the depths of your soul: When people criticize Zionism, they mean Jews—make no mistake about it.[17]

At an address at Brandeis University in 1967, King once again referred to the black-Jewish relationship: "The relations between Jews and Negroes are important because historically Jews have been intimately associated with the civil rights struggle and because as a people Jews are the most cohesive, consistent liberal force in American society."[18]

But racial strains were stretching the cords of brotherhood. Though some people could find some rationalizations for the now pronounced black hostility toward Jews, intellect could not replace the raw emotionalism of the exceedingly vitriolic black-Jewish interface. After one meeting he attended, Rabbi Harold Schulweis, an eminent congregational leader in Los Angeles, reported the vitriol that had come from a black member of the discussion group:

> You American Jews can't even imagine what it means to be humiliated, can you? Just don't fool yourself into forgetting that you're white. And don't tell me about slavery and Pharaoh and Egypt. That's three thousand years ago. I heard you describe how you use salt water instead of tears, and horseradish as a symbol of bitterness. Well, White Brother, we don't use symbols. We use tears for tears and the gall of our wretchedness is bitterness enough. And don't tell me about the success of your people and pulling yourself up by your bootstraps. Chains are not bootstraps, Brother. Don't compare yourself with us.[19]

Christian theologians also entered the fray, trying to calm the waters or at least explain why they were so turbulent. A. Roy Eckhardt, who had done so much to smooth the waters between Jews and Christians, wrote:

> As a means of combating hostility to Jews, the current educational literature of various Christian bodies often stresses that Jesus, who is reputed to have suffered "for the sake of" men, was himself a Jew. Without depreciating the good that this may do under generally favorable moral and spiritual conditions, we must not underestimate its opposite effect. We have to take into account the psycho-spiritual syndrome in accordance with which it is unconsciously held that because Jesus was a Jew, he really "had it coming." If the Christian's salvation "depends on the cross," ... this means that in a significant sense it depends upon the death of a Jew. But may this not open the way to a malicious logic, promulgated by sinful men or at least by distorted minds, that if this one Jew suffered to save us, cannot other Jews do the same? The line from Calvary to Auschwitz and the other death camps is in this respect one of simple geometrical progression: one Jew, six million.

This is why there is an important respect in which a Jew is able to claim Jesus of Nazareth with much less guile than the Christian is able to do. When Martin Buber testifies, "from my youth onwards, I have found in Jesus my great brother," he need not be embarrassed. Buber speaks as one Jew to another. When the Christian speaks this way, his testimony is stilled by the unstilled voices of the tormented Jews of Christian history.[20]

But with nothing quieting the assaults on Jews from some blacks, Jewish funds and support for civil rights groups dried up, and organizations such as SNCC soon found themselves without the resources to continue. They had hanged themselves with their own tongues.

Meanwhile, 1967 was not a good year for King, either. His own organization, the SCLC, was in disarray, black nationalists and radicals were ridiculing him as an Uncle Tom, and his politics, especially his attacks on United States involvement in Vietnam, were estranging him from former colleagues. Depressed and disheartened, King could only look forward to an uncertain 1968.

18

From One Battle
to Another

When the United States sent
military personnel to Viet-
nam in the late 1950s, it became involved with a mess that the French
had just previously been only too glad to leave. Not able to learn from
the Vietnamese defeat of the French, first President Dwight
Eisenhower and then President John F. Kennedy stuck their feet into
this quagmire. By the end of 1961, there were about 18,000 U.S.
troops in Vietnam. Though it seemed that Kennedy had finally realized the error of committing U.S. military to an Asian ground war, his
assassination in 1963 ended any hopes of a speedy American with-
drawal. Lyndon Johnson, who succeeded Kennedy as president, was
believed by some commentators to have had a psychological need to
prove that a poor Texan had more gumption than the Harvard blue
bloods of the Kennedy administration. Consequently, the United
States became even more deeply embroiled in the undeclared war.

For Martin Luther King, Vietnam was a moral sore point—one whose economic repercussions, which tested Johnson's premise that he could provide Americans with both "guns and butter," he saw as setting back the entire civil rights cause. Especially after receiving the Nobel Peace Prize, King had seen himself as a moral leader for the entire world rather than merely an American fighting for civil rights. What the United States was doing in Vietnam appalled both his pacifist and his economic sensibilities. He saw the insurgency against the government in South Vietnam as a warranted, nationalist revolt against an oppressive regime and the United States' aid to that government as coming close to neocolonialism.[1]

From almost all his advisers, King generally received the same advice: Be quiet about Vietnam. It would divert his influence away from civil rights to an issue of international relations. He would be watering down his credibility as well as his influence. But he persisted and called for peace talks with Hanoi, as well as the admission of China into the United Nations—another sticking point of American foreign policy.

Many Jews were also against the war. In his report to the Board of Trustees of the Union of American Hebrew Congregations in May of 1965, after Johnson had again upped the number of American troops in Vietnam, Rabbi Maurice Eisendrath condemned America's effort to "stroll the world like 'a star-studded Texas sheriff' to impose *our* brand of law and order upon the entire world." He supported a resolution calling for a negotiated settlement to the conflict. Six months later, in an address to the Union's General Assembly, Eisendrath cited a plea from the Pope for peace that he had issued at the United Nations and a *New York Times* editorial affirming the right of every American to dissent from the government's policies.

At that time, though, only a handful of Jewish leaders, notably Rabbi Jacob Weinstein, president of the Central Conference of

American Rabbis; Rabbi Abraham Joshua Heschel of The Jewish Theological Seminary; and Rabbi Roland Gittelsohn of Temple Israel in Boston, openly opposed the war.[2]

And for many Jews, opposing the war would well prove to be a two-edged sword. Johnson liked having things his way. If you disagreed with him, he was likely to find a sore point to which he could apply the pressure until you complied with his wishes. For Jews, Israel was that sore point. Never saying it outright, Johnson strongly implied to several key Congressional and Jewish leaders that Jewish opposition to the war could trigger cuts in American military and economic aid to Israel. It was a true trump card.

King, in the meantime, continued to insist that it was his moral duty to oppose the war. For this he had little support, even from within the SCLC. At the organization's annual convention in August 1965, King proposed that Johnson make an "unconditional and unambiguous statement" that would declare his willingness to negotiate with the North Vietnamese and their indigenous allies in South Vietnam. He also asked for both sides to demonstrate good faith: the United States would stop bombing the north, while the north would stop insisting that the United States immediately and unilaterally withdraw its forces. But delegates at the convention overwhelmingly defeated opposed King's proposal that he write a personal letter to Johnson; Ho Chi Minh, the head of North Vietnam; and U Thant, the secretary-general of the United Nations, to break the impasse. And during an SCLC board of directors meeting at the convention, Joseph Lowery, one of King's most faithful aides, worried that the SCLC was not "structured to go into this kind of complex, difficult and confusing area." His caution was echoed by Andrew Young, who affirmed that "we are as much against the war in Vietnam as anyone, but let us not abandon our tried and trusted methods of producing social

change to get on a bandwagon that's playing a 'square' tune." In addition, Bayard Rustin warned that if King did not stop campaigning
against the war, his opponents would come swarming down on him.[3]

Yet, despite the consensus among his advisors, King's attacks on
American involvement in Vietnam did not relent. As he told three
thousand people at an anti-war rally in New York City on April 4,
1967 at The Riverside Church, "Something said to me, 'Martin,
you've got to stand up on this. No matter what it means.'" After reading an article on the suffering of the children in Vietnam, he told
himself, "'Never again will I be silent on an issue that is destroying
thousands and thousands of little children in Vietnam.' I came to the
conclusion that there is an existential moment when you must decide
to speak for yourself; nobody else can speak for you."[4]

King delivered one of his most impassioned speeches against the
war, and certainly the most comprehensive statement he had ever given
for opposing it. He expressed his sympathy for the Vietcong and for revolutionary movements throughout the Third World. Communism, he
said, was primarily a revolt against the failures and injustices of capitalism, which had left a legacy of revolutionary nationalism. It was the
duty of the West to support these revolutions now, since the United
States had been the greatest purveyor of violence in the world.
Comparing American action in Vietnam to what the Nazis had done
during the Holocaust, he said that the United States should withdraw
from Vietnam, recognize the Communist-led National Liberation
Front, and pay war reparations for the damage done.[5]

The results of the speech were tumultuous. Bayard Rustin, a life-
long pacifist, broke with King because he felt that the problems of the
Negro were more important than concentrating on the injustices of a
foreign war. The Jewish War Veterans, which had long supported
King, attacked him for comparing the war in Vietnam to the
Holocaust. Rabbi Richard G. Hirsch, whose offices at the Reform

movement's Religion Action Center in Washington King had frequently used when visiting the capital, spoke for many anti-war clerics who could not support King's position: "We are not prepared to go
along with these people who think that everything the United States
does is wrong and everything Hanoi does is right."[6]

As King looked at his former comrades who were now turning
against him, he said to Levison that his cause was just, and like the
prophets of the Bible he understood that his position would be unpopular. Assuming the mantle of Hebrew prophet, King stood firm in his
nonviolent beliefs. As he had told the Synagogue Council of America
just two years before:

> The Hebrew prophets belong to all people because their concepts
> of justice and equality have become ideals for all races and civiliza-
> tions. Today we particularly need the Hebrew prophets because they
> taught that to love God was to love justice: that each human being
> has an inescapable obligation to denounce evil where he sees it and
> to defy a ruler who commands him to break the covenant.
>
> The Hebrew prophets are needed today because decent peo-
> ple must be imbued with the courage to speak the truth, to realize that
> silence may temporarily preserve status or security but to live with a
> lie is a gross affront to God. It is scarcely a secret that many congress-
> men, educators, clergymen, and leaders of national affairs are gravely
> disturbed by our foreign policy. A war in which children are incinerat-
> ed by napalm, in which American soldiers die in mounting numbers
> while other American soldiers, . . . in unrestrained hatred shoot the
> wounded enemy as they lie on the ground, is a war that mutilates the
> conscience. Yet important leaders keep their silence. I know this to be
> true because so many have confided in me that they shared my opin-
> ions but not my willingness publically [sic] to state them.
>
> The Hebrew prophets are needed today because we need
> their flaming courage; we need them because the thunder of their
> fearless voices is the only sound stronger than the blasts of bombs
> and the clamour [sic] of war hysteria. . . . In the days to come as the

> voices of sanity multiply we will know that across thousands of years
> of time the prophet's message of truth and decency, brotherhood
> and peace survives—that they are living in our time to give hope to
> a tortured world that their promise of the kingdom of God has not
> been lost to mankind.[7]

At the anti-war Spring Mobilization event of April 15, King marched with New Leftists who were marching under the banner of the Viet Cong flag. This only antagonized more people against King and convinced J. Edgar Hoover all the more that King was a Communist sympathizer.

On April 24, 1967, King joined Rabbi Maurice J. Eisendrath of the Union of American Hebrew Congregations, Philip Baum of the American Jewish Congress, and a few other religious and cultural leaders in announcing the formation of a new peace action group, Negotiation Now. The group would gather a million signatures on a petition asking for the United States to take further initiatives for a truce, for North Vietnam and the National Liberation Front to positively respond to these initiatives, and for South Vietnam to join these steps as well.[8]

Meanwhile, some civil rights groups and black groups had changed so much that they bore little resemblance to what they had been just a few years before. SNCC, for instance, deleted nonviolent from its name and advocated racial war in the United States. And a relatively new group, the Black Panthers, which had formed as recently as 1966, became a rallying point for particularly disaffected blacks. In an amalgam of socialism and black nationalism, the Panthers advocated black self-defense and the restructuring of American society to make it more politically, socially, and economically equal. They were armed and disciplined, and their tough persona made them especially appealing to the many blacks who felt humiliated and emasculated by white racism.[9]

King, in turn, tried to revitalize the SCLC with a Poor People's Campaign that would be held in Washington during the summer of 1968. We now know, but it was unknown to King at the time, that Lyndon Johnson and the director of the FBI were collaborating to ensure King's downfall.

19

End of the Dream:
Memphis

K ing's Poor People's March would focus on the poverty suffered by all people, not just blacks. The breadth of this multiracial effort would surpass the Washington March of 1963. It was scheduled for April 22, 1968, and King began a people-to-people tour to get the volunteers, the participants, and the money necessary to make the plan a reality.

But first came an urgent message from a friend in Memphis, James Lawson. The city's sanitation workers, most of whom were black, had attempted to form a union for better pay and working conditions. When their efforts were stymied by the mayor of Memphis, they went on strike. With tensions rising and threats of violence in the air, Lawson asked King to come to Memphis to move the issue onto a larger platform by his presence.[1]

As Andrew Young later said, "[W]hat had started out as a union grievance had . . . widened into a racial and civil rights struggle because the black community identified so strongly with the plight of the workers."[2]

Though deeply immersed in plans for the march in Washington, King felt that the issues involved in Memphis were similar to those involved with his Poor People's Campaign: People who wanted to make an honest living were being pushed down by a repressive system. So he went to Memphis, where he called for a protest march and general strike by workers and students.

But King had come into the situation without knowing all the details. Unknown to him, local youth groups did not support any of the more moderate black groups. Infatuated with the idea of Black Power, they were championing violence and revolution as a response to racism and discrimination. When King returned to Memphis a few weeks later to lead the march, rock-throwing, looting teenagers necessitated that the march be called to a halt. As King and Abernathy left the scene, rioting ensued. One hundred and fifty-five stores were damaged, sixty people were injured, and a sixteen-year-old black youth was killed by police gunfire. Mayor Loeb imposed a curfew, and the governor sent in thirty-five thousand National Guardsmen to patrol the city.[3]

King was distraught. In addition to being saddened by the loss of life, he knew all too well what his critics and the press would do with this debacle. Just when King was most in the doldrums, and as if by divine intervention, Lyndon Johnson, behind in the primary polls and overwhelmed by the deteriorating conditions in Vietnam, announced that he would not seek reelection. For King, this brought a new hope that change could take place, that America could be brought back to a readiness to heal its wounds.

Though still depressed by the recent events in Memphis, King returned again to the city to honor the commitment he had made to the sanitation workers. That night, King spoke of the Good Samaritan who stopped to help a man in need on the Jericho road. A main message of this parable (Luke 10:29-37) is that the traveller who helped the man in need was neither the priest, nor the Levite, a countryman of the victim. Rather, it was a foreigner who stopped and gave assistance. This seems a fitting parallel to King's work to assist the Jewish community: King helped the Jews just as the Good Samaritan helped the man in need to whom he had no ties—beyond the tie of human love. When King concluded, he stated some of the most eerily prophetic words ever recorded:

> Well, I don't know what will happen now. We've got some difficult days ahead. But it doesn't matter with me now. Because I've been to the mountaintop. And I don't mind. Like anybody, I would like to live a long life. Longevity has its place. But I'm not concerned about that now. I just want to do God's will. And He's allowed me to go up to the mountain. And I've looked over. And I've seen the promised land. I may not get there with you. But I want you to know tonight, that we, as a people will get to the promised land. And I'm happy, tonight. I'm not worried about anything. I'm not fearing any man. Mine eyes have seen the glory of the coming of the Lord.[4]

The next day, while on the balcony of his motel room, Martin Luther King was shot. Moments later he was dead. But that didn't stop the FBI from continuing to wiretap King's associates. One FBI report reveals a conversation that took place between Harry Wachtel and Stanley Levison shortly after King's death:

> It is indicated that Harry already knows that King is dead. They agree that it is sad. Stanley says [assassination] was always a possibility and yet none of "us" ever wanted to think of it. Harry says that the night of "the benefit" King stayed at Harry's place until very late that morning and that "we" talked about nothing else for two hours.... Levison says that about six months ago he told King that it was time that "we"

got some professional bodyguards. But Levison says one could never get King to really do it because it just ran against his grain. Levison says this is not only a personal tragedy of the whole movement because who else has what King had? Harry agrees, adding: "Not one other living human being." Levison agrees and adds, "white or black."[5]

Epilogue

"My people were brought to America in chains," Martin Luther King, Jr. told the American Jewish Congress' Biennial in 1958. "Your people were driven here to escape the chains fashioned for them in Europe. Our unity is born of our common struggle for centuries, not only to rid ourselves of bondage, but to make oppression of any people by others an impossibility."

Dr. King was expressing his certainty that Jewish and African American leaders could forge an alliance that would soundly defeat both racism and anti-Semitism. By the early 1960s Dr. King's message had inspired black and Jewish visionaries to further solidify bonds of friendship and brotherhood, bonds that would help define the history of the civil rights struggle in this country. By the late 1960s, however, tensions between the two communities had begun to obscure the invaluable work both groups had done in tandem to promote racial healing and harmony. And by the end of the century—three decades after the two Jewish civil rights workers Andrew Goodman and

Michael Schwerner were slain alongside James Chaney in Mississippi—some would be saying that the bedrock of common alliance had irretrievably crumbled, strewing the path to tolerance and justice with its rubble.

Fortunately, the lessons of the past have not been lost on many African American and Jewish leaders, on people of conscience who understand that simple human decency requires that forces be joined to vanquish intolerance and bigotry. And much has been done in recent years to repair the breach that has divided blacks and Jews. This work—which King would not only have endorsed, but would have led—is now bearing fruit. In the late 1990s, there was substantial cooperation between African Americans and Jews on the local and national levels. There were symposia, dialogues, joint celebrations of civic holidays and holy days, and joint visits by black and Jewish teenagers to sites that are historically significant for the civil rights struggle. Since 1997, there have been no significant, headline-generating disputes between mainstream African American and mainstream Jewish organizations.

In 1997, The Foundation for Ethnic Understanding conducted the first national poll ever taken on the state of black/Jewish relations in the United States. The poll revealed that African Americans and Jews agree far more than they differ. A majority of African Americans and Jews say the relationship between the two communities has improved in recent years.

In a sense, we have come full circle from the days when Dr. King admonished in his book, *Stride Toward Freedom*, "May the people of race in America soon make hearts burn. . . ." For, while we can readily acknowledge the long way American society has come since Rosa Parks refused to give up her seat on a public bus in Montgomery, Alabama, in 1955, we should not yet assume that the road to justice and equality is finally free of resistance and barriers.

Life in the United States is now calmer and safer for blacks and Jews than it was four decades ago; both groups enjoy unprecedented access to power and affluence and greater acceptance in the broader society. But we must persistently and knowingly measure the distance we have traveled, and not mistake that for the distance that remains. And we must always remember that the battle for human rights is a common one and a mutual one, a battle which, since it is defined by the very word "human," demands that all of us put our collective shoulders to the wheel of decency. In this way we can—together—achieve that most grand of goals: a world no longer tarnished by the slanders of bigotry or the disturbances of intolerance. A world, in other words, very much like the one envisioned by Dr. Martin Luther King, Jr.

Notes

Chapter 1

1. Clayborn Carson, "King Biographies II," 1996. Internet biography.
2. Milton R. Konvitz, *Bill of Rights Reader; Leading Constitutional Case*, 3rd ed. (Ithaca, N.Y.: Cornell University Press, 1965), 799.
3. Seth Cagin and Philip Dray, *We Are Not Afraid* (New York: Macmillan, 1988), 53–54.
4. Richard Hammer, "The Life and Death of Martin Luther King," *Midstream*, 5:5 (May 8, 1968), 8.
5. Carson, "King Biographies III," 1996. Internet biography.
6. Martin Luther King, Jr., "I Have a Dream," in James Melvin Washington, ed., *A Testament of Hope: The Essential Writings of Martin Luther King, Jr.* (San Francisco: HarperSanFrancisco, 1986), 217.
7. King, "I See the Promised Land," in Washington, 286.
8. Ibid., 288.
9. Clayborne Carson, *The Autobiography of Martin Luther King, Jr.* (New York: Warner Books, 1998), 335.

CHAPTER 2

1. Israel J. Gerber, "The Meaning of Freedom," *Jewish Heritage*, 7:1 (1964), 18.
2. Gerber, 20.
3. Leo Baeck, "The Meaning of Justice," *Central Conference of American Rabbis Journal*, 9:1 (1961), 13.
4. Edmund Winter, "Pidyon Shvuyim: The Neglected Mitzvah," *Conservative Judaism*, 24:3 (1970), 45.
5. Albert Vorspan and David Saperstein, *Tough Choices: Jewish Perspectives on Social Justice* (New York: UAHC Press, 1992), 135.
6. Emil L. Fackenheim, "Religious Responsibility for the Social Order: A Jewish View," *Central Conference of American Rabbis Journal*, 9:4 (1962), 3.
7. Bernard Mandelbaum, "A Jewish Response to Black Anti-Semitism," *Conservative Judaism*, 24:1 (1969), 26.
8. Everett E. Gendler, "War and the Jewish Tradition," in Menachem Marc Kellner, ed., *Contemporary Jewish Ethics* (New York: Sanhedrin Press, 1978), 209.
9. Ibid., 207.
10. Samuel G. Broude, "Civil Disobedience and Jewish Tradition," *Central Conference of American Rabbis Journal*, 12:4 (1965), 34.
11. Henry Hampton and Steve Fayer, *Voices of Freedom: An Oral History of the Civil Rights Movement from the 1950s through the 1980s* (London: Vintage, 1995), 186.

CHAPTER 3

1. Hedda Garza, *African Americans and Jewish Americans* (New York: Franklin Watts, 1995), 142.
2. James Baldwin, "The Harlem Ghetto," in *James Baldwin: Collected Essays* (New York: The Library of America, 1998), 49.
3. Richard L. Rubenstein, "The Politics of Powerlessness," *Reconstructionist*, 34:7 (1968), 7.
4. Murray Friedman, *What Went Wrong: The Creation and Collapse of the Black-Jewish Alliance* (New York: The Free Press, 1995), 148–149.

5. James A. Wax, "The Attitude of the Jews in the South toward Integration," *CCAR Journal*, 26 (June 1959), 18–19.

6. Harry Golden, *Mr. Kennedy and the Negroes* (Greenwich, Conn.: Fawcett, 1964), 155.

7. Leonard Dinnerstein, "Southern Jewry and the Desegregation Crisis, 1954–1970," *American Jewish Historical Quarterly*, 62:3 (1973), 238.

8. King, "The Un-Christian Christian," *Ebony*, 20:8 (1965), 79. Other rabbis in the South who fought racism included Jacob Rothschild of Atlanta, Georgia; Emmet Frank of Alexandria, Virginia; Allan Tarshish of Charleston, South Carolina; Malcolm Stern of Norfolk, Virginia; William Silverman of Nashville, Tennessee; and Ira E. Sanders of Little Rock, Arkansas.

9. John Slawson, "Letter to the Editor," *New York Times Magazine*, April 13, 1967.

10. Melissa Fay Greene, *The Temple Bombing* (Reading, Mass.: Addison-Wesley, 1996), 181.

11. Yaakov Landynski, "The Orthodox Jew as a Social Activist," *The Jewish Observer*, 8:6 (1972), 8.

12. Marvin Schick, "The Orthodox Jew and the Negro Revolution: A Hard Look at Religious Jewry's Attitudes," *The Jewish Observer*, 2:3 (1964), 15.

13. Arthur Hertzberg, et. al., "Changing Race Relations and Jewish Communal Service: A Symposium," *Journal of Jewish Communal Service*, 41:4, 333.

14. Arthur J. Lelyveld, "Negro and Jewish Relationships," *Congress Bi-Weekly*, 33:10 (1966), 9.

15. Hasia Diner, *In the Almost Promised Land: American Jews and Blacks, 1915–1935* (Baltimore: Johns Hopkins Press, 1977), 236–237.

16. Jonathan Kaufman, *Broken Alliance: The Turbulent Times between Blacks and Jews in America* (New York: Scribner's, 1988), 101.

CHAPTER 4

1. Arnold Shankman, "Friend or Foe?" in *Turn to the South: Essays on Southern Jewry*, Nathan M. Kaganoff and Melvin I. Urofsky, eds. (Charlottesville, Va.: University Press of Virginia, 1979), 123.

2. Eli N. Evans, *The Provincials: A Personal History of Jews in the South* (New York: Simon & Schuster, 1997), 270.

3. Richard Wright, *Black Boy* (New York: Harper & Row, 1945), 70–71.

4. Horace Mann Bond, "Negro Attitudes toward Jews," *Jewish Social Studies*, 27:1 (1965), 3–4.

5. King, in Washington, 202–203.

6. Carl Hermann Voss and David A. Rausch, "American Christians and Israel, 1948–1988," *American Jewish Archives*, 40:1 (1988), 53.

7. Reinhold Niebuhr, "The Relations of Christians and Jews in Western Civilization," *Central Conference of American Rabbis Journal*, 21 (April 1958), 29–30.

8. King, "Six Talks in Outline," *The Papers of Martin Luther King, Jr.: Vol. 1: Called to Serve, January 1929–June 1951* (Berkeley: University of California Press, 1992), 245.

9. Lewis V. Baldwin, *There Is a Balm in Gilead: The Cultural Roots of Martin Luther King, Jr.* (Minneapolis: Fortress Press, 1991), 327.

10. Samuel Newman, "Martin Luther King, Jr.," *The Jewish Spectator*, 33:6 (1962), 16–17.

11. Newman, 16–17.

12. King, "In Peace and in Dignity," *Congress Bi-Weekly*, 35:8 (May 6, 1968), 16–17.

13. King, *Where Do We Go from Here?* in Washington, 609–610.

14. King, "The American Dream," in Washington, 212.

15. "Eisenhower Plea for Negro Patience Assailed by Martin Luther King, Jr.," American Jewish Congress, May 15, 1958.

16. Newman, 16–17.

17. Ibid., 17.

18. Ibid., 16–17.

CHAPTER 5

1. "Joan Daves: Obituary," *The New York Times*, June 6, 1997.

2. Joseph Kirchberger ([husband of the late Joan Daves], telephone interview, Bedford, N.Y.) December 26, 1997.

3. Stephen B. Oates, *Let the Trumpet Sound: A Life of Martin Luther King, Jr.* (New York: HarperPerennial, 1994), 58.

4. Mark Bauman, "Introduction," in Mark K. Bauman and Berkley Kalin, eds., *The Quiet Voices: Southern Rabbis and Black Civil Rights, 1880s to 1990s* (Tuscaloosa: University of Alabama Press, 1997), 6.

5. Malcolm Stern, "The Year They Closed the Schools: The Norfolk Story," in Bauman and Kalin, 288.

6. Stern, 288.

7. Avi M. Schulman, *Like a Raging Fire: A Biography of Maurice N. Eisendrath* (New York: UAHC Press, 1993), 53.

8. Dinnerstein, 234.

9. Schulman, 53.

10. Ibid., 54.

11. William S. Malev, "The Jew of the South in the Conflict on Segregation," *Conservative Judaism*, 13:1 (1958), 45.

12. Vorspan, "Unease in Dixie: II. A Visitor's Account," *Midstream*, 2:4 (1956), 47.

13. Morris B. Abram interview, New York, October 27, 1997.

14. Abram interview.

15. Abram interview.

16. Martin Luther King, Sr. "Dear Senator," July 27, 1983. Special Collections Department, Robert W. Woodruff Library, Emory University, Atlanta, Georgia.

17. Andrew Young, *An Easy Burden: The Civil Rights Movement and the Transformation of America* (New York: HarperCollins, 1996), 265.

18. Marc Dollinger, " 'Hamans' and 'Torquemadas': Southern and Northern Jewish Responses to the Civil Rights Movement, 1945–1965," in Bauman and Kalin, 73.

19. Bond, 9.

20. Greene, 180.

21. Malev, 45.

22. Schulman, 554–55.

23. Vorspan, 49.

24. Oates, 107.

CHAPTER 6

1. Friedman, 308.
2. Ibid., 171.
3. David J. Garrow, *Bearing the Cross: Martin Luther King, Jr., and the Southern Christian Leadership Conference* (New York: William Morrow & Co., 1986), 83–84.
4. Kivie Kaplan, "Letter to Rev. Martin Luther King," March 29, 1962.
5. Friedman, 166.
6. Ibid., 172–173.
7. Garrow, 117.
8. Young, 266.
9. Friedman, 170.
10. Garrow, 116.
11. Alex Ayres, *The Wisdom of Martin Luther King, Jr.* (New York: Meridian, 1993), 139.
12. David L. Lewis, *King: A Critical Biography* (New York: Praeger Publishers, 1971), 131.

CHAPTER 7

1. Greene, 380.
2. Golden, "Jew and Gentile in the New South," *Commentary*, 20:5 (1955), 412.
3. Leonard Dinnerstein, *Antisemitism in America* (New York: Oxford University Press, 1994), 181–184.
4. Greene, 185–186.
5. Ibid., 187–188.
6. David Holzel, "Ahead of His Time," *The Atlanta Jewish Times*, April 17, 1992.
7. Bauman, 10–11.
8. P. Allen Krause, "Rabbis and Negro Rights in the South, 1954–1967," *American Jewish Archives*, 21:1 (1969), 38.
9. Dinnerstein, "Southern Jewry and the Desegregation Crisis, 1954–1971," 239.

10. Jacob M. Rothschild, "The Rabbi Will Serve No Good Purpose in Leading Crusades," *Central Conference of American Rabbis Journal*, 14 (June 1956), 5.
11. Greene, 188.
12. Ibid., 184–185.
13. Krause, 38.
14. Greene, 380.
15. Oates, 152.
16. Abram interview.
17. Harris Wofford, *Of Kennedys and Kings* (Pittsburgh: University of Pittsburgh Press, 1992), 14.
18. Coretta Scott King, *My Life With Martin Luther King, Jr.* (New York: Holt, Rinehart and Winston, 1969), 195.
19. Taylor Branch, *Parting the Waters: America in the King Years 1954–63* (New York: Simon and Schuster, 1988), 377.

CHAPTER 8

1. "Dresner Recalls Rights Fight: Sadness, Humor of Jail, Streets," *Hillel Scroll*, B'nai B'rith Rutgers-Douglass Hillel, December 1963, 1.
2. Rabbi Israel Dresner interview, Wayne, N.J., September 27, 1997.
3. Oates, 174.
4. Norman H. Finkelstein, *Heeding the Call: Jewish Voices in America's Civil Rights Struggle* (Philadelphia: Jewish Publication Society, 1997), 144–145.
5. Ibid.
6. King, "Address to the American Jewish Congress," May 15, 1958 (New York: Archives of the American Jewish Committee, Blaustein Library).
7. "Freedom-Riding Rabbi Says Southern Jews Begged Him Not to Endorse Integration," *Jewish Exponent*, December 7, 1962, 1.
8. Dresner interview.
9. "Springfield Rabbi Jailed with Freedom Riders," *The Daily Journal* (Elizabeth, N.J.), June 17, 1961, 1.

10. Milton Friedman, "Court Ponders Fate of Two Jersey Rabbis Before High Court," *American Jewish Life*, November 22, 1963, 1, 8.

11. "Freedom-Riding Rabbi . . ."

12. "Clergy Pray Way into Jail," *New York Herald Tribune*, August 29, 1962, 1–2.

13. "Freedom-Riding Rabbi . . ."

14. "Believes Jews Must Act in Opposition to Southern Bias," *The Jewish News*, September 14, 1962, 1.

15. Dresner interview.

16. Gary Gobetz, "Civil Rights Fighting Rabbi Urges Jewry to Take Lead," *The National Jewish Post and Opinion*, August 16, 1963.

17. King, Telegram to Rabbi Israel Dresner, August 5, 1964. From the files of Rabbi Israel Dresner.

18. Gunter David, "State Department Official Lauds Soviet Jewry Protest," *Newark (N.J.) Evening News*, September 20, 1965.

19. Rabbi Israel Dresner telephone interview, Wayne, N.J., March 11, 1998.

CHAPTER 9

1. King, as reported by Rabbi Marc H. Tanenbaum, "Address at the Ecumenical Service Commemorating the 51st Birthday of the Rev. Dr. Martin Luther King, Jr." at the Ebenezer Baptist Church, Atlanta, Georgia, January 15, 1980 (New York: Archives of the American Jewish Committee, Blaustein Library), 3.

2. Richard L. Rubinstein, "The Rabbis Visit Birmingham," *The Reconstructionist*, 29:8 (1963), 6.

3. Greene, 180.

4. Gobetz.

5. Ibid.

6. Terry Barr, "Rabbi Grafman and Birmingham's Civil Rights Era," in Bauman and Kalin, 176–177.

7. Arthur M. Schlesinger, *Robert Kennedy and His Times* (Boston: Houghton Mifflin, 1978), 330.

8. Oates, 216.

9. Dollinger, 71.

10. Jack Greenberg, *Crusaders in the Courts* (New York: Basic Books, 1994), 334–335.

11. Friedly and Gallen, 183.

12. "White Clergymen Urge Local Negroes to Withdraw from Demonstrations," *Birmingham News*, April 13, 1963, 2.

13. King, "Letter from Birmingham City Jail," in Washington, 293, 294–295.

14. Ibid., 299.

15. Dollinger, 75.

16. William M. Kunstler with Sheila Isenberg, *My Life as a Radical Lawyer* (New York: Birch Lane Press, 1994), 127–128.

17. Oates, 237.

18. In fact, nineteen rabbis actually made the trip: Arnie Becker, Memphis, TN; Jacob H. Bloom, Fairfield, CT; Kenneth Bromberg, Pittsburgh, PA; Moshe Cahana, Houston, TX; Moshe Davidowitz, Greenwich, CT; Morris Fishman, Margate, NJ; Isaac Freeman, Newburgh, NY; Seymour F. Friedman, Spring Valley, NY; Everett Gendler, Princeton, NJ; Stanley M. Kessler, West Hartford, CT; Richard L. Rubinstein, Pittsburgh, PA; Moses B. Sachs, St. Louis Park, MN; Sidney D. Shanken, Cranford, NJ; Alexander Shapiro, Philadelphia, PA; Paul Teicher, Trenton, NJ; Andre Ungar, Westwood, NJ; Eugene Weiner, Hamilton, Ontario, Canada; Richard W. Winograd, Chicago, IL; and Harry Z. Zwelling, New Britain, CT.

19. Eli N. Evans, *The Provincials: A Personal History of Jews in the South* (New York: Simon & Schuster, 1997), 286–87.

20. Andre Ungar, "To Birmingham and Back," *Conservative Judaism*, 8:1 (1963), 13.

21. Richard L. Rubenstein, "The Rabbis Visit Birmingham," *The Reconstructionist*, 29:8 (1963), 6–7.

22. Ibid., 8.

23. Evans, *The Provincials*, 287.

24. Jack Bloom, "Journey To Understanding," *Conservative Judaism*, 19:4 (1965), 16.

25. Barr, 185.

26. Vorspan, telephone interview, New York, November 12, 1997.

Chapter 10

1. Jervis Anderson, *Bayard Rustin: Troubles I've Seen* (New York: HarperCollins, 1997), 239.

2. Richard G. Hirsch, "Toward a Social Theology for Social Action," *CCAR Journal*, 15:1 (1968), 72–73.

3. Benjamin J. Kahn, "The Jewish Community and Civil Rights," Jewish Heritage, 7:1 (1964), 23.

4. David Danzig, Telegram to Charles Wittenstein, American Jewish Committee, August 14, 1963 (New York: Archives of the American Jewish Committee, Blaustein Library).

Fourteen Jewish organizations signed a nationally publicized document endorsing the march on Washington: the American Jewish Committee, the American Jewish Congress, the Anti-Defamation League of B'nai B'rith, the Central Conference of American Rabbis, the Farband Labor Zionist Order, the Jewish Labor Committee, the Jewish War Veterans, the Rabbinical Assembly of America, the Rabbinical Council of America, the Union of American Hebrew Congregations, the Union of Orthodox Jewish Congregations of America, the United Hebrew Trades, the United Synagogue of America, and the Workmen's Circle. "14 Major Jewish Groups Endorse Aug. 28 March on Washington," *The Southern Israelite* (Atlanta, Ga.), August 23, 1963, 1.

Even after the march, the American Jewish Committee still had to reassure its membership that it had done the right thing: "[T]he drive for equality is not solely a Negro problem. It is a challenge calling for moral commitment and decisive action by Americans of every race and religion and of every section of the country. It is increasingly clear to whites as well as Negroes that gradualism and 'tokenism' will no longer solve this most urgent of all domestic problems." Irving M. Engel, Chairman, Committee on Race Relations, "Draft Statement on AJC and Negro Protest," The American Jewish Committee, October 24, 1963 (New York: Archives of the American Jewish Committee, Blaustein Library).

5. As quoted in Anderson, 256.
6. Finkelstein, 154.
7. "March on Washington Hears Two Rabbis as Thousands of Jews Take Part," The Southern Israelite (Atlanta, Ga.), September 6, 1963, 1.
8. As quoted in King, Address in Acceptance of the Solomon Schechter Award, United Synagogue Biennial Convention, November 1963.
9. King, in Washington, 219–220.

CHAPTER 11

1. Branch, Pillar of Fire, 120.
2. Ibid.
3. Cagin and Dray, 219.
4. Kaufman, 47–48.
5. David Harris, Dreams Die Hard: Three Men's Journey through the Sixties (San Francisco: Mercury House, 1993), 47.
6. Sanford Wexler, The Civil Rights Movement: An Eyewitness History (New York: Facts On File, 1993), 202.
7. Milton Viorst, Fire in the Streets: America in the 1960s (New York: Simon and Schuster, 1979). William Chafe, Never Stop Running (New York: Basic Books, 1993), 264.
8. Chafe, 451, 460. David Harris, Dreams Die Hard (New York: St. Martin's Press, 1982), 2, 324.

CHAPTER 12

1. Samuel H. Dresner, "When Paul Robeson Sang the 'Kaddish' in Moscow," The National Jewish Monthly, 80:4 (1965), 14.
2. Martin Bauml Duberman, Paul Robeson (New York: Alfred A. Knopf, 1988), 352–353.

3. Dresner, 15. Duberman, 353.

4. Duberman, 353–354, 711–712.

5. Lewis H. Weinstein, "Soviet Jewry and the American Jewish Community 1963–1987," *American Jewish History*, 77:4 (1988), 600.

6. William Korey, *The Soviet Cage* (New York: Viking Press, 1973), 80, 161. Theodore Freedman, *Anti-Semitism in the Soviet Union* (New York: Freedom Library Press of the Anti-Defamation League, 1984), 555.

7. Wendy Eisen, *Count Us In: The Struggle to Free Soviet Jews, a Canadian Perspective.* (Toronto: Burgher Books, 1995), 16.

8. King, "Speech to United Synagogue of America Golden Jubilee Convention Upon Receipt of the Solomon Schechter Award," *New York Journal American* (November 20, 1962), 30 (New York: Archives of the American Jewish Committee, Blaustein Library).

9. Weinstein, 600.

10. "A Bleak Prospect for Russian Jewry," editorial, *The Reconstructionist*, 29:11 (October 4, 1963).

11. "An Appeal of Conscience for the Jews of the Soviet Union," Conference on the Status of Soviet Jews, October 12, 1963 (Waltham, Mass.: American Jewish Historical Society Archives).

12. Weinstein, 605.

13. Abraham Heschel, "What Happens to Them Happens to Me," in Jack Salzman, et al., eds., *Bridges and Boundaries: African Americans and American Jews* (New York: The Jewish Museum, 1992), 86–87.

14. Weinstein, 602.

15. Nahum Goldmann, Letter to Mr. Lewis H. Weinstein, Geneva, March 7, 1964 (New York: Archives of the American Jewish Committee, Blaustein Library).

16. King, "What Happens to Them Happens to Me," in Salzman, 88.

17. King, Letter to the *Times*, *The New York Times* (January 16, 1965).

18. King, Response to Award of the American Civil Liberties Medallion, American Jewish Committee Annual Meeting, May 20, 1965 (New York: Archives of the American Jewish Committee, Blaustein Library).

19. "U.S. Negro Leader Urges Americans to Protest Soviet Policy on Jews," *Daily News Bulletin, Jewish Telegraphic Agency*, 32:112 (June 11, 1965), 2.

20. "Eternal Light Vigil Highlights Soviet Union's Bias Against Jews," *Daily News Bulletin, Jewish Telegraphic Agency*, 32:181 (September 20, 1965), 2.

21. Roy Wilkins, "A Negro Leader Pleads for Soviet Jewry," *The National Jewish Monthly*, 80:10 (1966), 12.

22. King, Address on Soviet Jewry Human Rights Day, December 11, 1966 (New York: Archives of the American Jewish Committee, Blaustein Library).

CHAPTER 13

1. Oates, 293.
2. Ibid.
3. Ruth Silberstein, "A Southern Rabbi Takes a Stand," *Congress Weekly*, 25:2 (1958), 7.
4. Harry I. Baron, Address Before Jewish Community Relations Council of St. Louis, May 31, 1962 (Waltham, Mass.: Archives of the American Jewish Historical Society).
5. Kunstler, 136–137.
6. Kunstler, 137–138.
7. Arnold Jacob Wolf, "The Negro Revolution and Jewish Theology," *Judaism*, 13:4 (1964), 478–479.
8. Branch, 354.
9. Rabbi Allen Secher, telephone interview, Chicago, Ill., December 3, 1997.
10. Vorspan, "In St. Augustine," *Midstream*, 10:3 (1964), 16–17.
11. Kunstler, 138
12. Vorspan, 18.
13. Ibid.
14. Branch, *Pillar of Fire*, 355.
15. Ibid., 355–356.

16. Vorspan, telephone interview, New York, November 12, 1997.

17. Branch, *Pillar of Fire*, 356.

18. Rabbi Joel S. Goor, "Twenty-Four Hrs. in a St. Augustine Jail," *The Southern Israelite* (July 10, 1964), 4.

19. Oates, 299.

20. Kunstler, 138–139.

21. Vorspan interview.

CHAPTER 14

1. Heschel, *The Wisdom of Heschel*, selected by Ruth Marcus Goodhill (New York: Farrar, Straus & Giroux, 1977), 175.

2. Finkelstein, 147.

3. Heschel, *Israel: An Echo of Eternity* (New York: Farrar, Straus & Giroux, 1969), 113.

4. Branch, *Pillar of Fire*, 22–23.

5. Heschel, *The Wisdom of Heschel*, 70.

6. Ibid., 177.

7. Heschel, "Racism Is Satanism," from the *United Synagogue Review*, as printed in *The Southern Israelite* (September 13, 1963), 4.

8. Branch, *Pillar of Fire*, 31–32.

9. Ibid.

10. Susannah Heschel, "God and Society in Heschel and King," online, The Shalom Center, Internet, February 24, 1998.

11. A. Heschel, *The Wisdom of Heschel*, 167.

12. S. Heschel, "Heschel As Mensch," in Neusner and Neusner, 205–206.

13. Branch, *Pillar of Fire*, 168. King, address at UAHC convention, Chicago, November 20, 1963.

14. S. Heschel, "Introduction," in Susannah Heschel, ed., *Abraham Joshua Heschel, Moral Grandeur and Spiritual Audacity: Essays* (New York: Farrar, Straus & Giroux, 1996), xxiii–xxiv.

15. Ibid.

16. Ibid.

17. A. Heschel, as quoted by Tanenbaum, "Address at the Ecumenical Service."

18. "Conversation With Martin Luther King," in Washington, 658–659.
19. Finkelstein, 164.
20. A. Heschel, as quoted in Tanenbaum, "Address at the Ecumenical Service."
21. Peter Geffen telephone interview, January 9, 1998.

CHAPTER 15

1. Greene, 415.
2. Oates, 337.
3. Greene, 418–419.
4. Ibid., 422.
5. Rabbi Jacob Rothschild, Tribute, Atlanta Dinner honoring Nobel-Winner Dr. Martin Luther King, Jr., January 27, 1965 (Atlanta, Ga.: King Library).
6. Oates, 326.
7. Hampton and Fayer, 212.
8. Oates, 343.
9. Bruce Perry, *Malcolm: The Life of a Man Who Changed Black America* (Barrytown, N.Y.: Station Hill Press, 1992), 348–349. Branch, *Pillar of Fire*, 579.
10. Thomas R. Peake, *Keeping the Dream Alive* (New York: Peter Lang, 1984), 267.
11. Branch, *Pillar of Fire*, 580.
12. Ibid., 583.
13. Ibid., 587.
14. Ibid., 599.
15. Ibid., 753. Oates, 346.
16. Tanenbaum, "Address at the Ecumenical Service."
17. "Jewish Groups Protest to Johnson on Anti-Negro Action in Alabama," *Daily News Bulletin, Jewish Telegraphic Agency*, 32:4 (1965), 4. The seven agencies that joined the NCRAC in the telegram to the President were the American Jewish Congress, Jewish Labor Committee, Jewish War Veterans, National Council of Jewish Women, Union of American

Hebrew Congregations (Reform), Union of Orthodox Jewish Congregations of America, and United Synagogue of America (Conservative). Among the Jewish clerics who were in Selma were Sol Berman, California; Maurice Davis, Indianapolis, IN; Israel Dresner, Springfield, NJ; H. Bruce Ehrmann, Brockton, MA; Maurice Eisendrath, New York, NY; Albert Hoschander Friedlander, New York, NY; Joseph Gumbiner, Berkeley, CA; Abraham Heschel, New York, NY; Richard Hirsch, Washington, DC; David Levy, California; Lipnick and Sigel of St. Louis, MO; Gerald Raiskin; Mathew Simon, Los Angeles, CA; and David Teitelbaum and Joseph Weinberg, California.

18. Greenberg, 356–357.
19. Harry S. Ashmore, *Civil Rights and Wrongs: A Memoir of Race and Politics 1944–1994* (New York: Pantheon Books, 1994), 174.
20. Don G. Lebby, Letter, March 20, 1965 (New York: Archives of the American Jewish Committee, Blaustein Library).
21. Friedlander, 26–27.
22. Finkelstein, 162.
23. Oates, 365.
24. "Selma's Agony and Ours," American Jewish Committee *Newsletter*, 1:1 (1965) (New York: Archives of the American Jewish Committee, Blaustein Library).
25. King, Speech to Adas Israel Congregation, Washington, D.C., August 1965 (New York: Archives of the American Jewish Committee, Blaustein Library).

CHAPTER 16

1. Robert G. Weisbord and Richard Kazarian, Jr., *Israel in the Black American Perspective* (Westport, Conn.: Greenwood Press, 1985), 22.
2. "Israel and the U.S. Black Community: An Information Program to Improve Attitudes," Department of Urban Affairs, Ruder & Finn, Inc. (New York: December, 1968), 3–4 (New York: Archives of the American Jewish Committee, Blaustein Library).
3. Branch, *Parting the Waters*, 44.

4. Carl Hermann Voss and David A. Rausch, "American Christians and Israel, 1948–1988," *American Jewish Archives*, 40:1 (April 1988), 53.

5. Therion E. Cobbs, "I Saw Israel's Miracle," *The Jerusalem Post* (December 1, 1966).

6. King, "The Death of Evil upon the Seashore." Sermon delivered at the service of prayer and thanksgiving, Cathedral of St. John the Divine, Washington, D.C., May 17, 1956. In Clayborne Carson, ed., *The Papers of Martin Luther King, Jr. Vol. III, Birth of a New Age, December 1955–December 1956* (Berkeley: University of California Press, 1997), 260.

7. Young, 417–418.

8. Irving Spiegel, "8 Church Leaders Ask Aid to Israel," *The New York Times*, May 28, 1967. The ad in the *Times* on June 4, 1967, read: "Men of conscience must not remain silent at this time. The Middle East is on the brink of war. President Nasser of Egypt has initiated a blockade of an international waterway, the Straits of Tiran, Israel's sea lane to Africa and Asia. This blockade may lead to a major conflagration.

The Middle East has been an area of tension due to the threat of continuing terrorist attacks, as well as the recent Arab military mobilization along Israel's borders. Let us recall that Israel is a new nation whose people are still recovering from the horror and decimation of the European holocaust.

We therefore call on the United States government steadfastly to honor its commitments to the freedom of international waterways. We call on our fellow Americans of all persuasions and groupings and on the administration to support the independence, integrity and freedom of Israel.

Men of conscience all over the world bear a moral responsibility to support Israel's right of passage through the Straits of Tiran.

The people of Israel have the right to live and develop in tranquility and without fear. The Middle East requires respite and peace.

'Seek peace and pursue it.' (Psalms, 34:15)"

9. Friedman, 251.

10. Brant Coopersmith, "War in the Middle East," Memo to Harry Fleischman, The American Jewish Committee, June 12, 1967 (New York: Archives of the American Jewish Committee, Blaustein Library).

11. Arthur J. Lelyveld, "Negro and Jewish Relationships," *Congress Bi-Weekly*, 33:10 (May 23, 1966), 8–9.

12. Richard L. Rubenstein, "The Politics of Powerlessness," *The Reconstructionist*, 34:7 (May 17, 1968)

13. King, "Letter to an Anti-Zionist Friend," *Saturday Review*, 47 (August 1967), 76. Reprinted in King, *This I Believe: Selections from the Writings of Dr. Martin Luther King, Jr.* (New York, 1971), 234–235.

14. Friedman, 251, 252.

15. Nathan C. Belth, *A Promise to Keep* (New York: Times Books, 1979), 231–232.

16. Press Release, The American Jewish Committee, New York, October 10, 1967 (New York: Archives of the American Jewish Committee, Blaustein Library).

17. Press Release, The American Jewish Committee, October 10, 1967.

18. King, Letter to Morris B. Abram, President American Jewish Committee, September 28, 1967 (New York: Archives of the American Jewish Committee, Blaustein Library).

19. "Anti-Semitism, Israel, and SCLC: A Statement on Press Distortions," *SCLC Newsletter*, September 1967.

20. Friedman, 252–253.

21. Washington, 670.

22. Eckhardt, 10–11.

23. King, "I See the Promised Land," in Washington, 284–285.

CHAPTER 17

1. "Of Riots and Wrongs Against the Jews," *SCLC Newsletter*, July–August 1964, 11.

2. King, address at UAHC convention, November 20, 1963.

3. *Playboy* interview as quoted in Washington, 370.

4. Leonard Dinnerstein, *Antisemitism in America* (New York: Oxford University Press, 1994), 209.

5. Dinnerstein, 209–210.

6. Dinnerstein, 210.

7. Dinnerstein, 210. Friedman, 267.

8. Stanley Levison and Amram Nowak, "Background Memorandum and Suggested Program for the Metropolitan Council, American Jewish Congress on Negro-Jewish Relationships," June 5, 1963, 3–5 (Waltham, Mass.: Archives of American Jewish Historical Society).

9. Friedman, 227–228. Kaufman, *Broken Alliance*, 80–81.

10. Hampton and Fayer, 294.

11. King, "Comments at Rabbinical Assembly Convention, 25 March 1968," in Washington, 668–669.

12. Will Maslow, "Negro and Jew in America," *World Jewry*, 7:1 (1964), 9.

13. M. C. Gettinger, Minutes of Atlanta Jewish Community Council, Community Relations Committee, December 21, 1966 (Atlanta, Ga.: Archives of the Atlanta Federation).

14. King, "My Jewish Brother," *Amsterdam News*, February 26, 1966, 1,12.

15. Charles E. Silberman, "Negro and Jewish Relationships," *Congress Bi-Weekly*, 33:10 (1966), 7.

16. Friedman, 227–228. Kaufman, 80–81.

17. King, "Letter to an Anti-Zionist Friend," *Saturday Review*, 47 (August 1967), 76.

18. King, "Can There Be One America," Address at the President's Inauguration, Brandeis University, Waltham, Mass., October 4, 1967.

19. Harold M. Schulweis, "The Voice of Esau," *Reconstructionist*, 31:16 (1965), 7–8.

20. A. Roy Eckardt, "Theological Approaches to Anti-Semitism," *Jewish Social Studies*, 33 (1971), 277 (footnote).

Chapter 18

1. Friedman, 243–244.

2. Schulman, 58–59.

3. Friedman, 244. Adam Fairclough, *To Redeem the Soul of America: The Southern Christian Leadership Conference and Martin Luther King, Jr.* (Athens, Ga.: The University of Georgia Press, 1987), 271.

4. King's April 4, 1967, speech at Riverside Church. In Clayborne Carson, *The Autobiography of Martin Luther King, Jr.* (New York: Warner Books, 1998), 335.

5. Ibid., 246–247.

6. Jim Bishop, *The Days of Martin Luther King, Jr.* (New York: Putnam's, 1971), 466.

7. King, An Address at the Synagogue Council of America, Waldorf-Astoria Hotel, December 5, 1965.

8. *Jewish Currents*, 21:6 (1967), 46.

9. "Black Panther Party," www.Africana.com. Film review of "Panther" in *Socialist Review*, Issue 191, November 1995.

CHAPTER 19

1. Oates, 470.

2. Young, 448.

3. Oates, 477.

4. King, "I See The Promised Land," in Washington, 286.

5. Friedly and Gallen, 598.

Index

Abernathy, Ralph David 38, 61, 71, 190
Abram, Morris Berthold 41, 44, 66, 153, 171
Achim, Ahavath 61
ADA. *See* Americans for Democratic Action
ADL. *See* Anti-Defamation League
Adler, Morris 136, 168
Alexander, Cecil and Hermie 65
Ali, Muhammad 177
Allen, Ivan, Jr. 59, 145–146
American Jewish Committee
  award to King from 117
  Israel and 163–164
  leadership of 153
  publication of 20, 157
  Southern blacks and 26
  Soviet Jews and 115
  Washington March and 94–95, 95 n. 4
American Jewish Conference of Soviet
    Jewry 115, 117
American Jewish Congress
  leadership of 26, 176, 186
  Levison and 173
  publication of 177
  Southern Jews and 24
  Washington March and 95 n. 4, 96–97
American Nazi Party 149

Americans for Democratic Action (ADA)
  104
Anderson, Marian 97
Anti-Defamation League (ADL) 24, 26,
  95 n. 4, 167
Anti-Semitism
  Dresner on 74–75
  King and xiv, 172, 177
  in Russia 107–120
  See also racism.
Atlas, Seymour 24, 40, 95 n. 4
B'nai B'rith. *See* Anti-Defamation League
Baeck, Leo 12
Baker, Ella Jo 50–51, 53
Baker, Wilson 147, 149
Baldwin, James 20, 99
Baldwin, Louis 32
Barnett, Ross 101–102
Baron, Henry 123
Bates, Daisy 97
Baum, Philip 186
Becker, Arnie 88 n. 18
Belafonte, Harry 52, 81
ben Zakkai, Jochanan 14
Berman, Sol 153 n. 17

Bevel, James and Diane Nash 87, 97, 148, 151–152, 156
Blachschleger, Eugene 45
Black Panthers 186
Black Power xiv, 190
Bloom, Jack 90–91
Bloom, Jacob H. 88 n. 18
Böll, Heinrich 37
Bond, Horace Mann 30–31, 45
Borders, William Holmes 60
Borowitz, Eugene 127–128, 130
Branch, Taylor 138
Brickner, Balfour 127
Brock, James 126
Bromberg, Kenneth 88 n. 18
Brotherhood of Sleeping Car Porters 93
Broude, Samuel 15
Brown v. Board of Education 4, 22–23, 62
Brown, Clifford 176
Brown, Esther 22
Brown, Oliver 22
Brown, Robert McAfee 72
Buber, Martin 89, 180
Bunche, Ralph 139
Cahana, Moshe 88 n. 18
Canetti, Elias 37
Capitol Press Club 164
Carmichael, Stokely 175
CCAR. See Central Conference of American Rabbis
Central Conference of American Rabbis (CCAR) 86, 94–96, 95 n. 4, 126, 129, 182–183
Chaney, James 101–103
civil rights 20, 81
  in Atlanta 59–68
  Heschel and 133–143
  Jews and 20, 70
  legislation 8, 81, 130–131
  protest 7–8, 11, 95
  religion and 13
  tactics 6, 60, 100
  voting and 148
  war and 9
  whites involved in 6–7, 23, 101
  See also King on civil disobedience and civil rights.
Clark, Jim 147, 149, 152–155
Cobbs, Therion E. 160
Coffin, William Sloane 140
COFO. See Council of Federated Organizations

Collier, John W. P. 72
Collins, Leroy 154
Committee on Equal Opportunity in Housing 113
communism 32, 49–50, 54–55, 111
Conference for New Politics 167–168
Conference of Presidents of Major American Jewish Organizations 113, 115
Conference on Religion and Race 142
Congress of Racial Equality (CORE) 8, 70, 100–101, 175–176
Conley, Jim 58
Connor, Eugene 78–79, 83, 87–88, 139, 148
Cooper, Annie Lee 149
CORE. See Congress of Racial Equality
Council of Federated Organizations (COFO) 100–103
Danzig, David 95 n. 4
Davidowitz, Moshe 88 n. 18
Davis, Joan 37, 171
Davis, L. O. 121, 129
Davis, Maurice 153 n. 17
Dayan, Moshe 177
Decter, Moshe 112–113
Diner, Hasnia 26
discrimination
  in education 22
  Jews and 19–27
  Soviet Jews and xiv
  See also segregation.
Douglas, William O. 114
Dresner, Israel 69, 71–75, 125, 127, 153 n. 17, 171
Dresner v. Tallahassee 69, 75
DuBois, W. E. B. 159
Dulles, Allen 102
Eastland, James 97
Ebenezer Baptist Church 2, 5
Eckhardt, A. Roy 169, 179
Ehrmann, H. Bruce 153 n. 17
Einstein, Albert 117
Eisendrath, Maurice J. 39–40, 46–47, 153 n. 17, 156, 171, 182, 186
Eisenhower, Dwight D. 47, 181
Elias, Joel 22
Ellington, Duke 52
Epstein, Elias 42
Epstein, Harry H. 61–61
Evans, Annie 124–125
Fackenheim, Emil 13
Farband Labor Zionist Order 95 n. 4

Farmer, James 104
Faubus, Orville 63
Federal Bureau of Investigation (FBI) 6,
    186, 191
Feffer, Itik 109
Fishman, Morris 88 n. 18
Flagler, Henry 121
Foyer, Leon 96
Frank, Emmet 24 n. 8
Frank, Leo 41
Freedman, Karl 90
Freedman, Martin 71–75
Freedom Rides and marches 69–76, 145–158
Freeman, Isaac 88 n. 18
Friedlander, Albert Hoschander 153 n. 17,
    155
Friedman, Murray 51, 163, 166
Friedman, Seymour F. 88 n. 18
Gaston, A. G. 81
Gendler, Everett 14, 88 n. 18
Gerber, Israel 11
Glazer, Nathan 173
Golden, Harry 23, 57
Goldmann, Nahum 115
Goldstein, Benjamin 39
Goldstein, Israel 113
Goldstein, Jerold 127
Goldstein, Marvin G. 61
Goldwater, Barry 8, 97
Goodman, Alfred L. 24
Goodman, Andrew 101–102, 172, 193
Goodman, Carolyn and Robert 103
Goor, Joel S. 127, 130
Gorbachev, Mikhail 120
Grafman, Milton 82, 85–86, 91
Greenberg, Jack 23, 82, 150, 171
Gumbiner, Joseph 153 n. 17
Hallinan, Paul J. 145
Hardge, Arthur L. 72
Hartmire, Wayne, Jr. 72
Hartsfield, William B. 59–60, 66–67
Hass, Joe and Betty 65
Hayling, Robert B. 121
Hellman, Yehuda 113
Henry, Aaron 104
Hertzberg, Arthur 25
Heschel, Abraham Joshua 99, 112, 116,
    133–143, 153 n. 17, 155, 171, 183
Heschel, Susannah 137, 140
Hesse, Herman 37
Heston, Charlton 96
Hirsch, Richard 71–72, 94, 153 n. 17, 184

Ho Chi Minh 183
Holocaust, the 34, 134
Hoover, J. Edgar 6, 55, 186
Humphrey, Hubert 99, 104, 151
Innis, Roy 175
Israel 76, 159–179
Jackson, Jesse 97
Jackson, Jimmy Lee 151–152, 154, 156
Jackson, Mahalia 97
Jackson, Robert 42
Jackson, Samuel 167
Javits, Jacob 97
Jenkins, Herbert 59
Jewish Labor Committee 95 n. 4, 153 n. 17
Jewish Minorities Research 112
Jewish War Veterans 95 n. 4, 153 n. 17, 184
Judaism
    blacks and 19, 27, 30–31, 78–91, 102,
        116–118, 179–180
    Conservative 16, 25, 88. See also
        Rabbinical Assembly of America;
        United Synagogue of America.
    in Israel 159–170
    in Montgomery, Alabama 38–47
    northern and southern 24–25 39–41, 47,
        61–65
    Orthodox 16, 25. See also Rabbinical
        Council of America; Union of
        Orthodox Jewish Congregations of
        America.
    prophetic 86, 140
    Reform 16–26, 70, 94. See also Central
        Conference of American Rabbis;
        Union of American Hebrew
        Congregations.
    social justice and 16–17
    Soviet xiv, 75, 107–120
John XXIII 136
Johnson, Frank 153, 155
Johnson, Lyndon Baines 7–8, 102,
    104–105, 114, 131, 152–154,
    153 n. 17, 158, 162, 181–183, 187, 190
Jones, Clarence 151
Kaplan, Kivie 51
Katz, Harold 79
Katzenbach, Nicholas 148, 151, 153
Kaufman, Jonathan 27, 102
Kennedy, John F. 6–7, 66, 68, 81, 91,
    97–98, 114, 181
Kennedy, Robert F. 68, 81
Kessler, Stanley M. 88 n. 18
Khrushchev, Nikita 113, 115
Kichko, Trofim 111

King, Albert Daniel 2, 88, 91
King, Christine 2
King, Coretta Scott 3, 50–51, 65–67, 150, 170
King, Edwin 104
King, Martin Luther, Jr.
  arrest of 5, 8, 41, 66, 73
  assassination of 10, 170, 191
  awards 7, 8, 117
  books, writings
    "Birmingham Manifesto" 82
    "Letter from Birmingham City Jail" 6
    "Stride Toward Freedom" 5
    "Why We Can't Wait" 6, 76
  childhood 1–3, 31, 37–47
  education of 31, 160
  Heschel and 133–143
  Levison and 55
  on bigotry 172, 177
  on black anti-Semitism 172, 177
  on Catholic power 175
  on civil disobedience 1–2, 10, 14–15, 23, 34, 85, 158,185
  on civil rights xiii, 164
  on cooperation of religions 158
  on CORE 70
  on equality 185
  on heroism 75, 185
  on Heschel 141–142
  on his vocation 191
  on the Holocaust 34
  on hope 33, 36
  on Israel 160–161, 165–166, 168–169, 178
  on Jesus 32
  on Jews xiii–xiv, 11, 27, 31, 33–35, 45, 116–117, 127, 160–161, 165–166, 168–169, 171, 175, 178
  on justice 1–2, 10, 185
  on love of neighbor, 170
  on nonviolence 5, 75
  on peace in Middle East 169
  on power 175
  on prophets 32, 185
  on psychology 172
  on racism 70–71, 171, 194
  on sectarianism 36
  on segregation 5, 33, 45, 77–78, 158, 172, 185
  on slavery 34, 165, 193
  on social action 34, 158
  on Soviet Jewry 116–117
  on Vietnam war 184–185
  on war (not addressing) 164, 184–185
  on Zionism 165–166, 168–169, 178
  papal visit by 8
  passive resistance and 5
  politics and 8
  ridicule of 180
  scripture and 32
  Southern rabbis and 24
  speeches
    "I have a dream" 7, 97–98
    "I've been to the mountaintop" 9–10, 191
    "The Good Samaritan" 170
  stabbing of 47
  State of Israel and xiv
  surveillance of 6, 55, 186, 191
  voting rights and 8
  Vietnam and 8–9, 180–181
  war and 75
King, Martin Luther, Sr. (Daddy King) 1–2, 44, 59, 66–68
Kinoy, Arthur 53
Ku Klux Klan (KKK) 130, 147, 156
Kunstler, William 87, 124–128, 171
Lane, Mills B., Jr. 59
Lawson, James 189
Lazarus, Emma 160
LDF. See Legal Defense Fund
Lebby, Don G. 155
Leby, Richard 127
Legal Defense Fund, NAACP's (LDF) 23, 82, 150
Lehman, Herbert H. 114
Lelyveld, Arthur 26, 103, 172
Levison, Stanley 44, 49–56, 83, 163, 166, 171, 173–174, 185, 191–192
Levy, David 153 n. 17
Lewis, John 97, 148, 152, 154
Lincoln, Abraham 7
Lingo, Al 150–151
Lipman, Eugene 127, 154
Lipnick 153 n. 17
Liuzzo, Viola 156
Loeb, Mayor 190
Lowenstein, Allard 99–106
Lowery, Joseph 183
Maislan, George 96
Malcolm X 150, 173
Malev, William 40, 45
Mandelbaum, Bernard 13, 88
Mantinband, Charles 23–24
Manucy, Hoss 121–123, 128–130
Marshall, Burke 88

Marshall, Thurgood 23
Martin, Louis 172
Maslow, Will 176
Mays, Benjamin 2, 145
McCarthy, Eugene 105
McCarthy, Joseph 50
McGill, Ralph 145
McKinney, Petty D. 72
Memphis, Tennessee 189–193
MFDP. *See* Mississippi Freedom
    Democratic Party
Mikhoels, Solomon 109
Miller, Irving 113
Miller, Uri 96
Minkoff, Isaiah M. 113
Mississippi Freedom Democratic Party
    (MFDP) 103–105
Mistral, Gabriela 37
Mitchell, Oscar 68
Montgomery Improvement Association 4
Moses, Bob 100
NAACP. *See* National Association for the
    Advancement of Colored People
Nasser, Gamel Abdel 162 n. 8
National Association for the Advancement
    of Colored People (NAACP)
  COFO and 100
  LDF of 23, 82, 150, 175
  leadership of 2–3, 22, 82, 117, 122, 150
  schools and 22–23
  SCLC and 52, 122
  SNCC and 175
  voting and 53
National Catholic Welfare Conference 74
National Community Relations Advisory
    Council 153
National Conference of Christians and
    Jews 136
National Conference on Religion and
    Race 74, 77
National Council of Churches of Christ 74
National Council of Jewish Women
    153 n. 17
National Jewish Community Relations
    Advisory Council (NJCRAC) 113–114
National Liberation Front 186
National States' Rights Party 125
Neely, Frank 59
Neibuhr, Reinhold 3, 31, 137, 160, 162
Nixon, E. D. 4, 67
Nixon, Richard M. 67–68
NJCRAC. *See* National Jewish Community
    Relations Advisory Council

Nkrumah, Kwame 47
nonviolence
  children and 87–88, 99
  passive resistance 5, 149–159
  scorned 9
  See also civil disobedience; King on
      nonviolence.
Nussbaum, Perry E. 24
Oates, Stephen 38
Orris, Peter 16
Parks, Rosa 4, 97, 194
Paul VI 8, 136, 182
Peabody, Malcolm and Mary 124
Phegan, Mary 58
Pizitz, Louis 80–81
Plaut, Walter 71–72
Plessy v. Ferguson 3, 22
Polier, Shad 96
Porter, John T. 91
Powell, Adam Clayton 55
President's Conference of Jewish
    Organizations 115
Prinz, Joachim 97
Pritchett, Laurie 73
Pushkin, Alexander 108
Rabbinical Assembly of America 95 n. 4
Rabbinical Council of America 95 n. 4
racism
  in Atlanta 145
  Jews and 29, 36
  King and xiv, 70–71, 75, 172, 177, 194
  in St. Augustine 121–131
Raiskin, Gerald 153 n. 17
Randolph, A. Philip 47, 50, 93–94, 97, 117
Rauh, Joseph 104–105
Rauschenbusch, Walter 2–3
Ray, Sandy 162
Reagan, Ronald 44
Reeb, James 154
Reuther, Walter 105, 114
Rich, Dick 59, 65
Richardson, Gloria 97
Robeson, Paul 108–111
Rockwell, George Lincoln 149
Rodell, Marie 38
Roosevelt, Eleanor 124
Roosevelt, Franklin Delano 42
Roosevelt, Theodore 114
Rosenberg, Julius and Ethel, 49
Rosenwald, Julius 22
Roth, Dora 90
Rothschild, Bill 63

Rothschild, Jacob 24 n. 8, 62–63, 65,
145–147
Rothschild, Myron J. 39–40
Roy, Ralph Lord 72–73
Rubinstein, B. T. 127
Rubinstein, Richard L. 88 n. 18, 89, 165
Rustin, Bayard 50–55, 93, 105, 117, 184
Sachs, Moses B. 88 n. 18
Sachs, Nelly 37
St. Augustine, Florida 121–132
Samstein, Mendy 105
Sanders, Ira E. 24 n. 8
Schick, Marvin 25
Schneier, Arthur 116
Schulweis, Harold 179
Schwerner, Michael and Rita 101,
103–104, 172, 194
SCLC. See Southern Christian Leadership
Conference
Scott, Coretta. See Coretta Scott King.
Secher, Allen 127
sectarianism 30, 36
segregation
in Atlanta 57–58
in Burmingham 77–92
on buses 4–5
in the courtroom 73
in Florida 33
legislation 22–23
in Montgomery 38–39
See also King on segregation.
Selma, Alabama 145–158
Shanken, Sidney D. 88 n. 18
Shapiro, Alexander 88 n. 18
Shimon bar Yochai 14
Shriver, Sargent 67
Shur, Moshe 143
Shuttlesworth, Fred 77, 79–80, 128–129
Sigel 153 n. 17
Silberman, Charles 177
Silverman, William 24 n. 8, 123
Simon, Mathew 153 n. 17
Simpson, 131
Skankman, Arnold 29
Slaton, John 58
slavery 5, 34, 165, 193
Slawson, John 24
Smitherman, Joe 147
Smyer, Sidney 80
Soviet Jewry xiv, 75, 110–120
SNCC. See Student Nonviolent
Coordinating Committee

social justice
allegiance to country 14
conservative Jews and 16
involvement and 13–14
Jewish tradition and 11–16
love and 13, 20
monotheism and 12
Orthodox Jews and 16
politics and 13
Reform Jews and 16
silence about 23–24
See also civil rights; King on civil rights.
Southern Christian Leadership
Conference (SCLC)
CORE and 8
FBI and 6
finances of 9, 161, 180
formation of 5, 52–53
importing protesters 124, 149
Jews and 79, 88, 161, 167–168, 171
leadership of 55, 77, 82, 122–123, 148
Malcolm X and 150
Poor People's Campaign 187
SNCC and 8, 168
students and 65
war and 183
Spiegel, Irving 162 n. 8
Spotswood, Stephen Gill 162
Springarn, Arthur 22
Stern, Malcolm 24 n. 8
Stone, Robert J. 72, 130
Stoner, J. B. 125, 149
Student Nonviolent Coordinating
Committee (SNCC) 8, 65, 97, 100,
148, 151, 154, 163, 168, 171,
174–175, 177, 180, 186
Sweeney, Dennis 105–106
Synagogue Council of America 26, 74, 96,
185
Tarshish, Allan 24 n. 8
Teicher, Paul 88 n. 18
Teitelbaum, David 153 n. 17
Thant, U 183
Thomas, Norman 105
Tillich, Paul 2
Ungar, Andre 88 n. 18, 89 n.20, 90
Union of American Hebrew Congregations
24, 26, 70, 95 n. 4, 153 n. 17, 154,
156, 182, 186
Union of Orthodox Jewish Congregations
of America 95 n. 4, 153 n. 17
United Hebrew Trades 95 n. 4
United Synagogue of America 95 n. 4, 96,
112, 138, 153 n. 17

Vandiver, Ernest 57
Vatican II 136
Vietnam 8–9, 180–181, 184
Vivian, C. T. 122–123
Vorspan, Albert 126, 128, 131
Wachtel, Harry 151, 171, 191
Wallace, George C. 152–156
Warner, A. McArven 72
Warren, Robert Penn 114
Wechsler, James 105
Weil, Rosetta 65
Weinberg, Joseph 153 n. 17
Weiner, Eugene 88 n. 18
Weinstein, Jacob 182
Weinstein, Lewis H. 114
Wieman, Henry Nelson 2
Wilkens, Roy 47, 104, 117

Williams, Adam Daniel 2
Williams, Alberta 2
Williams, Hosea 123–125, 148, 152, 176
Winograd, Richard W. 88 n. 18
Wittenstein, Charles 95 n. 4
Wofford, Harris and Clare 51, 54, 66
Wolf, Arnold Jacob 126
Woodruff, Robert W. 146
Workmen's Circle 95 n. 4
World Jewish Congress 115
Wright, Richard 30
Yarrow, Peter 106
Yitzhak, Levi 107–110
Young, Andrew 44, 105, 125, 150, 162–163, 165, 183, 189
Zionism 159–170
Zwelling, Harry Z. 88 n. 18

About **JEWISH LIGHTS** Publishing

People of all faiths and backgrounds yearn for books that attract, engage, educate and spiritually inspire.

Our principal goal is to stimulate thought and help all people learn about who the Jewish People are, where they come from, and what the future can be made to hold. While people of our diverse Jewish heritage are the primary audience, our books speak to people in the Christian world as well and will broaden their understanding of Judaism and the roots of their own faith.

We bring to you authors who are at the forefront of spiritual thought and experience. While each has something different to say, they all say it in a voice that you can hear.

Our books are designed to welcome you and then to engage, stimulate and inspire. We judge our success not only by whether or not our books are beautiful and commercially successful, but by whether or not they make a difference in your life.

We at Jewish Lights take great care to produce beautiful books that present meaningful spiritual content in a form that reflects the art of making high quality books.

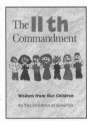